Secrets of a Kept Woman

2

SHANI GREENE-DOWDELL

Nayberry Publications | Nayberry Productions

Also by Shani Greene-Dowdell

Novels

Keepin' It Tight

Secrets of a Kept Woman 1

Short Stories

Lord Why Does It Feel So Good?

Before the Clock Strikes Twelve

Multi-Author Anthologies

Mocha Chocolate: Taste a Piece of Ecstasy
Mocha's Chocolate

Mocha Chocolate: Escapades of Passion
Baby Girl 1 and 2

Savor: The Longest Night
Love My Pain Away

Nayberry Publications
P.O. Box 1001
Opelika, AL 36803

NayberryPublications.com

Printed in the United States of America

First Edition: March 2014

Nayberry Publications is an independent press operating out of Opelika, Alabama. The Nayberry Publications name and logo is a trademark of Nayberry Publications, LLC.

Authors of Nayberry Publications are available for speaking events, book signings, and book club gatherings. To find out more, go to www.nayberrpublications.com or call 334.787.0733.

The publisher is not responsible for websites (or their content) that are not owned by the publisher.

ISBN 13: 978-0-9815843-8-6
ISBN 10: 0-9815843-8-1
LCCN: Application in Progress

To my supportive and loving husband:
Anthony Dowdell

Through all of these years, I appreciate you
being by my side through good and bad times.
I pray that God continues
to hold our marriage together in love.

Thanks for the great times and advice.

I love you

Always

Acknowledgements

There are many people that I thank for being a part of the success of the first novel in this series, Secrets of a Kept Woman 1. I will attempt to do justice to people who helped make it a best seller.

First of all, thank God for allowing me to see that no matter what obstacles the world is able to put up, He is able to turn any situation around. I remain faithful and believe, with all my heart, that with the faith of a mustard seed all of things God has destined will come to pass.

To my husband, I stood by your side as you dealt with health issues and I admire your strength. After 19 years of marriage, I am still learning who you are, as I am sure you are learning me. I appreciate the love and growth you have shown over the years. Thanks for encouraging me to finish this book.

To my children, Kim, Athena, and Anthony, thanks for being the loves of my life. Always remember that you can do anything you put yoru mind to. The world is yours! I pray for growth and progress in your young lives.

To my mother, sister, and brother, you believe in my dreams and encourage me to be a better. It's always good to look out and see that you are there when I need you. I love you all. Mama, thanks for your undying support. It's great to have you by my side.

To the cast and crew of the Secrets of a Kept Woman play, you helped bring an idea to fruition with little means. You did it with love and for that I appreciate you.

I am forever grateful to everyone who reads my work. Readers, book clubs, book sellers, and anyone with a love for literature, I salute you and encourage you to continue to support the Secrets of a Kept Woman series. The next book in the series is "You Can't Help Who You Love."

With love and joy,
Shani

Email: info@nayberrypublications.com
Facebook: www.facebook.com/shanibooks
Twitter: www.twitter.com/shaniwrites
Text @addme to 3347870733 to be notified about new releases

$\mathcal{P}$rologue

There comes a time in every woman's life when she must put herself first. Once Shayla Davis made the choice to place more value on her own happiness than other people, her life finally moved in the right direction. Sitting in her office, her beautiful, cocoa skin basked in the radiant glow of her recent choices. After being boxed in a hole six years ago, she came out swinging like a champ.

All of those years ago, when she walked into the den and found her best friend sucking on her husband's manhood, as if it contained the bread of life, she was devastated. As if that sordid affair wasn't enough, the nuclear war button was pressed when she found out the two were expecting a child. The fact that her husband's first child was growing inside of her best friend's womb was a swift kick in the gut.

For years, intuition told her he was not a faithful man. However, she was not prepared to find out the other woman was Rhonda Jackson. The memories loomed over her like a dark cloud. They were as vivid in her mind, as if it was yesterday.

'I loved you like a sister' she said to Rhonda when confronting her about sleeping with Titus.

The look in Rhonda's eyes was cold as ice. 'What's love got to do with it? This is not about love. This is about me getting what I want and I want Titus.'

'Go wait for me in the car, Rhonda!' Titus yelled as he pushed her toward the door. 'Why in the hell did you come in here, Ronnie?'

'It's hot in that damn car and I'm ready to go, so you need to make this snappy.' Rhonda snapped her fingers and rolled her eyes at him.

'Just go wait in the car!' Titus said. The second time it was more of a demand than a request.

'You got me waiting in the car like I'm some kid who can't go in the store. I'm not going back out there! Let's go now," Rhonda demanded.

'You better do what he says and get out of my house, Rhonda!' Shayla said as she rushed toward Rhonda, ready to attack her, but Titus held her back.

Rhonda shook her head in pity of her old friend. She took two steps toward the door, and then did a one hundred and eighty degree turn on the heels of her red bottom stilettos. A devious smile spread across her face. Rubbing her barely bulging stomach, she said, 'I will go for now. But, Titus is coming with me.'

Shayla took off her earrings and threw them on the floor. 'If you do not get out of my house, I will put you out, and since you want him so bad, take his trifling ass with you.'

'Whatever, bitch! We will all go. Me, Titus, and the baby!' Rhonda said and stormed out of the front door.

Her words were a dagger and she didn't stay to watch them hit the mark.

Shayla doubled over as if she'd been hit directly in the heart. Pain ripped through every inch of her body as she began to cry.

Attempting to console her, Titus said, 'I don't know what she's talking about. That baby is not mine.'

'Get out! Just please, get out!' she said as she pushed them both out of her house, heart and her mind.

It took months for her to come to terms with the reality of being divorced, but she eventually did.

Following the advice of her mother, she submitted an application to medical school and to her surprise she was accepted and started less than a year later. She took courses for pre-med when she was in college in her twenties, but decided to settle for a Bachelors in social work when she started dating Titus. He told her that spending ten years in college would be a waste of time. He said he had enough money to take care of them. So much for listening to a man like him for advice. She found out the biggest waste of time was taking his last name.

After graduating from medical school, she began her psychiatry residency at Emory University. She soon married Antonio Davis, a kind, loving, and supportive man, who was her rock and fire. He encouraged her to soar higher than her wildest dreams. In her newfound love and career, she found light at the end of the tunnel.

Chapter 1

Shayla

Shayla had enough work on her desk to keep her busy through the night. Shuffling through the mountain of files on her desk, she located her roster of patients for the day. It was already nine o'clock, so she mapped out a plan to get a full day of office work, hospital rounds, and her second year residency work done.

"I won't complain," she said in a sing-song melody, thinking back to the many times she heard her mother sing the song. She was so engrossed in her thoughts that she was startled when her phone vibrated in her pocket. She took it out and looked at the caller ID. It was Antonio. Her lips spread into an immediate smile.

"Hello," she said, delighted.

"Hello sweetie, I was sitting here thinking about you and wondering if I could take you out to dinner tonight." His sultry voice was deep and thick. All man.

5

She loved when he called her sweetie. There was something about the way his Hispanic accent rolled off his tongue into the word that made it special.

"That sounds nice, honey, and I would love to, but I have a lot of paperwork that I need to catch up on tonight." She looked at the many papers scattered on her desk wishing she could twinkle her nose and make it all go away.

"Come on, baby. It's Friday, I just got paid and I'm ready to hit the town."

She laughed, flattered that her husband still wanted to date her after so many years of being together. She said, "With the new health insurance laws rolling out, I have to make sure I have my ducks in a row. How about another time?"

"Since you will be gone all weekend, we wouldn't be able to go out until next week." He paused as if thinking about what he would say next. "The least you can do before you leave me at home, *all alone*, is let me take you out and show you a good time."

"I am not leaving you home alone. Did you forget about our handsome son? I am sure he will keep you company."

"I know he will, but..."

The line went silent for a long while and Shayla looked at her phone to make sure the call didn't drop.

"Hello?" she said.

Antonio let out a deep sigh. "I'm here."

"Stop doing that."

"What?"

"I can hear you clicking your pen, which is something that you do when you are upset. And even though I cannot see you, I am willing to bet that your eyebrows are wrinkled."

"I wouldn't be doing that if my wife would let me take her out tonight."

"How about we do something super special when I get home tonight? You know, just you, me, hot oils, and lingerie."

"Mrs. Davis, I would love that. But am I such a bad man for wanting to go out with my best friend in this cold and lonely world?"

She stopped shifting through the files and pushed the one in front of her to the corner of her desk. "No," she answered, smiling. It felt good to be Antonio's wife.

"This could be our final moment together. Do you want to spend it denying your husband a dinner date? You remember what I told you about final moments?"

"Yes," Shayla said recalling their wedding vows. "We vowed to live every moment like it is our final moment." She stood up and walked to the window. In the midst of deadlines, appointments, and health law requirements, the view from her office window was so calming. Watching the hustle and bustle of cars headed in many different directions somehow helped her see things more clearly. "Okay, I'm in, but who is going to watch Tyler? We need to get a sitter."

"I've already called Janessa. She is coming over at seven."

"So, you already knew I would give in, huh?"

He laughed that sexy laugh that she loved to hear. "You're my wife. I'm supposed to know your next move."

"Then you know the moves I'm going to put on you tonight then?"

"I am definitely trying to find out, woman. What time do you want me to pick you up?"

Shayla pulled the folder she moved earlier back to the center of her desk. "Around seven would be good. I have some things I have to finish up tonight. Plus, I'll need time to freshen up."

"No worries. Seven it is. I love you."

"I love you more." Shayla hung up the phone with Antonio, she dialed Lissa.

Lissa's company, Naytek Corp, shared office space with Shayla's office, Peach Psychiatric Services. The two ladies were traveling to Baltimore the next morning for a business conference. She wanted to make sure they both were on the same page.

Lissa answered on the second ring. "Hey, lady!"

"Hi, Lissa. I will be at your house around 6:45 in the morning, so we'll have plenty time to get through airport security and board the plane."

"I'll be ready," Lissa said confidently.

"You say that every time, and then when I get to your house I have to wait at least thirty minutes for you to get ready," Shayla said in a playful tone, but she was serious about leaving on time for the Baltimore trip. "We really have to be on time tomorrow. If we have to reschedule our flight, we may miss most of the conference."

"Oh, trust and believe, I have no plan to be late for this Naytek-sponsored trip to the Baltimore! I have big plans for the weekend."

"Like what?"

"To work a little and play a lot." A loud pop sounded through the phone and Shayla knew Lissa popped a piece of gum. "If you know what I mean."

"You and that chewing gum! Jesus, please, be a fence around some unsuspecting man this weekend. Protect him from Lissa, and whatever devious plan she has up her sleeve," Shayla said, shaking her head. "In the holy name of Jesus. Amen."

"You should be praying for Jesus to send my Boaz," Lissa replied and popped her gum even louder, knowing the noise worked Shayla's last nerve.

"I hope you don't end up on a milk carton before the weekend is over."

"I will never go out like that. Don't worry, I got this!"

Shayla let out a deep breath. "That's what I'm worried about."

"Hey, I have a meeting in ten minutes about the software implementation I told you about last week. I'll be ready at 6:30 in the morning, so no worries. My bags are packed and I'm ready to go."

Shayla picked up the healthcare reform newsletter that was lying on her desk. "Okay, see you then. Good luck with you project and please, take that gum out your mouth before you go into your meeting."

Before hanging up the phone, Lissa said, "Yes ma'am."

Shayla finished reading the newsletter, and then began writing notes in each file like a woman on a mission. Her husband expected her to be ready by seven, and she didn't plan to let him down. He was right. They didn't know what tomorrow would bring. Therefore, they would spend that day as if it was their last moments together. The more she thought about him, the more she couldn't wait to see him that evening. With a supportive husband, handsome son, prospering career, and beautiful home, she knew her life was beautifully and bountifully blessed.

As she examined her new life, she felt she was the true definition of a kept woman. She was kept by the power of God. He kept her sane and virtuous through turmoil. He kept her whole in a world of broken people.

"God, gave me victory in the end," she said with her eyes toward the heavens. "And for that, I thank you."

After signing off on a few more office files, she gathered her purse. She scrolled through the calendar app on her cell phone to see how many appointments she had scheduled for the upcoming week. Most of the clients were regulars, a few were new, but one particular name stood out like a gay wedding in the heart of the conservative south

That person was none other than her ex-best frenemy, Rhonda Wilson. "What is her name doing on my schedule?" she asked, and then looked back to the heavens. "Ok, Jesus. Now, I really need you to be a fence."

Chapter 2

Shayla

Shayla pushed the thought of seeing Rhonda's name on her client list to the back of her mind as she walked into Kinbrook Hospital. She headed straight to the psychiatry department. As a second-year resident, she was happy to get more responsibilities as a doctor and looked forward to assisting her patients. She stopped by the nurses' station to get updates before making rounds.

Once in the hall, she took the chart off, Ms. Prichette Morris' door. The past six months, and especially the past month, had been difficult. Her mental health situation came to a head when neighbors witnessed her wielding a gun at the cable guy who disconnected her services.

When she was brought into the hospital, she denied the entire incident and immediately began to play the role of the victim. The only person she would speak to was Shayla. To any of the other staff, she was practically mute.

After a knock, Shayla entered the room while calling out, "Hello? Ms. Morris?" When she got no answer, she proceeded with caution finding the tall and slender old woman sitting on the bed folding and unfolding a blue shirt. A pair of bright red pants was spread across the bed. The room was tidy, but Ms. Morris was outright disheveled. Her clothes were mismatched. Her hair stood straight up on her head in a tall afro.

"There you are!" Shayla said to her. Gesturing toward the clothes the woman had in her hand, she asked, "Are you going somewhere?"

Hope shined bright in the woman's eyes as she sat up straight in the bed. "Not unless you are letting me out of this crazy house."

"Well, that depends," Shayla said as she rocked forward on her heels. "How are you feeling today?"

"Dr. Davis, darling, I'm doing fair, I guess. I have missed you being here, though."

Shayla stopped flipping through the notes in her hand and raised an eyebrow. "But, I was just here yesterday."

"I know, but when you are not here, people are mean to me, so I missed you."

"In what way are people being mean to you? What do you mean?"

The woman's voice went from hopeful to furious in a matter of seconds. "Well, for starters, they brought me some old, nasty, dried up turkey for dinner last night and the so-called black eye peas were ghastly. I will not eat food that should be thrown out to the dogs. I am not a dog! I need to get out of here and go home, so I can eat like a human being." Ms. Morris stormed to the closet and put her shirt and pants inside her overnight bag. "I want to leave here, now!"

"Okay. I understand you have a problem with the food menu. However, considering how you presented, that is the least of our worries. Tell me what you would like to have for dinner today and I will see if I can get you something better to eat."

"I would like to be in my own home cooking my own dinner." The woman sat in a chair beside the bed and folded her arms.

"You have to have at least one day of improvement before we can consider that."

Ms. Morris wringed her hands together as if she was in deep thought. "That's a bunch of bull, but I'll take some chicken, macaroni and cheese, and broccoli on my dinner tray this evening. Yeah, that would be quite fine. That would be *very* good, actually."

"I will see if I can get that for you."

"Well, now that we have the menu settled, I feel so much better about my current situation." Ms. Morris's voice was dripping with sarcasm. "At least someone is working on important things around here."

Shayla's jaw tightened as she attempted to ignore Ms. Morris' sly remarks. "How did you sleep last night?"

"Slept pretty good to be in a hospital bed, I 'spect."

"See you do have good news. A good night's sleep is great! As far as getting home, I want to be able to write orders for you to go home. I do. However, it would help if you would communicate with the other staff."

"They talk to me like I'm some kind of dummy, so I act like one."

"Ms. Morris..."

"They do and that's that. I'm not talking to any of these rude fools."

"It would be great if you would meet me halfway. Your nurse told me there was commotion in your room last night and you were seen responding to voices."

Ms. Morris rolled her eyes to the sky and folded her arms tighter.

"Have the voices changed any since you started taking your new medication?" Shayla asked.

"Dr. Davis, the voices are getting louder and the visions are so clear. The thing I remember most is the eyes." The woman stood up from the chair and floated to the edge of the bed. She sat down and began to rock back and forth as she traveled to a place far away. "I started seeing them when I was seven."

"Did you tell anyone what you saw?"

"Only my friend, Lana. I asked her one time did she see eyes watching us from the trees. She said, 'No, Prichette! And stop being so creepy all the time.'

"She looked at me like I was as crazy as a Bessie bug, so I stopped mentioning the looming eyes to her. Instead, when I saw them, I packed my toys and rushed back home to my mama."

"Did you tell your mother about what you saw?"

14

"I didn't find a safety net in being at home with mama. 'Cause mama didn't believe in ghosts, scary eyes, or nothing like that. That is why as soon as she tucked me in for bed each night, the eyes came rushing from under my bed and stalked me like a tormented beast. Oh, they scared me silly, because they knew mama wouldn't come running to hear no stupid ghost stories." Ms. Morris shook as she spoke. Her fear was palpable in the air.

Shayla touched her arm. "We don't have to talk about this if it is too traumatic for you, Ms. Morris."

"It is terrifying at times. But, my visions aren't always bad ones, ya know? Sometimes the spirits are nice."

"Have you experienced any of the *nice* visions over the past week?"

Ms. Morris shoulders moved up and down as she laughed. "When Harriett appeared in the darkness, I was suddenly a part of one of her rescue missions. We went to the old Johnson plantation in Alabama. You ever heard of the Johnson slaves?"

Shayla hadn't heard of them. More importantly, she didn't know what the slave family had to do with Ms. Morris' current condition. She shook her head. "No. I haven't. However, you didn't answer my question."

"Well, it's not a big plantation. It had a big, pretty white fence with those big white columns on the porch though. Harriett greeted the Johnson slaves saying, 'Come along now. We gotta wait down by the big oak tree until more slaves is gathered.'

As Ms. Morris continued her story, Shayla wrote notes about her progress and current regress. She also clicked on her laptop to fill in some of the chart information that she had to complete for her assessment. She couldn't help but feel hopeless when it came to Ms. Morris. Even with her taking her meds, she often slipped out of touch with reality.

Realizing Shayla was not giving her 100% of her attention, Ms. Morris paced the room chanting, "No justice, no peace! No justice, no peace." Seconds later, her chanting came to an abrupt stop and she said, "And like I told you before, someone is taking my disability check. I just know it!"

She pointed her finger at Shayla and said, "I'm beginning to think that you're in on it since you can't tell me who is taking my check!"

"Ms. Morris, you're going to have to calm down. I know you don't like to be sedated, so please settle down."

Ms. Morris cut her eyes at her before sitting down. "I'm calm," she said as slow and measured as she could muster.

They talked for the next fifteen to twenty minutes about her living situation and some things that may have triggered her breakdown. At Ms. Morris' insistence, they also discussed her disability check and Shayla assured her that she had checked into the situation and that no one stole her check.

"Ms. Morris when social work called yesterday to check on your missing disability check, they were told by the disability office that your check is being deposited directly into your bank account. They also verified that the last three deposits transmitted to your bank account successfully. Unless someone has access to your banking account, the money should be in your account."

The woman let out a sigh of relief. "I didn't think to call the bank. I've just been waiting for the check to come in the mail like it used to. Now that you mention it, I set it up to go to the bank." She sat down in the chair and smiled. "Thank you."

"You're welcome." Shayla's face softened. "I am not going to be here this weekend but, if you have a good weekend, I think you will be okay to go home with supervision Monday. I will ask your brother to come in and meet with us for a family session before making that decision. Until then, be sure to take the medications Dr. Gray prescribed."

The woman picked up her shirt off the bed and rung it in her hands again. "I will," she said as she opened the shirt wide and folded it.

Shayla raised a warning eyebrow. "Take them without a fight."

"Sure will, sugah." Although her voice was as sweet as sugar, ambivalence was written all over her face.

Ms. Morris looked up from ringing her hands and said, "Thanks for being such a good person, Mrs. Davis. Never forget, Martin Luther King left his light on earth to shine in each and every one of us, so shine bright like a diamond."

With a slight grin, Shayla said, "Yes ma'am." Once in the hall, she smiled and shook her head. She hoped she could help Ms. Morris find a peace of mind. She wished she could wave a magic wand and mental illness all around the world would disappear.

Chapter 3

Antonio

Antonio rushed home from work, showered, and changed into a nice pair of jeans and gray dress shirt. He planned to take his wife to a comedy show and then out to a swanky Italian restaurant for dinner.

Janessa arrived on time and was in the living room playing with two-year-old Tyler. Antonio walked into the room and said, "I'm about to head out. Call my cell if you need anything. I don't want Shayla to worry about anything while we are out."

"We will be fine. Isn't that right Tyler Wiler?" Janessa assured as she squeezed Tyler's cheeks, causing him to laugh and blush.

"I am so happy that we have you around to help with Tyler. He loves you. Thanks for coming on such short notice."

"I am happy to be here. I love this little guy, too," she said with a big smile.

19

Antonio picked up his keys and walked toward the front door confident that his son was in loving hands. The home phone rang as he put his hand on the door knob. His first instinct was to ignore it and let Janessa answer it, but he said, "I'll get it." He turned and walked into the kitchen and retrieved the portable phone.

The caller ID displayed Gladys LaQuinn's number. Gladys was the third part to the trio of friends. Back in high school, Shayla, Rhonda, and Gladys were inseparable. Unlike Rhonda, Gladys remained loyal, true, and to that day, she and Shayla were the dearest of friends. Having escaped the hands of her physically abusive husband around the same time Shayla left Titus for sleeping with Rhonda, their bond grew tighter.

"Hey Gladys, what's up?" Antonio asked as soon as he pressed the answer button.

"Hey. How are you?" Her greeting was warm.

"I'm doing well."

"That is good to hear. You sound like you are in a rush. Did I catch you guys at the wrong time?"

"Something like that," he said, looking at the keys in his hand. "But, it's okay. What's up?"

"Is Shayla around?"

"No, I'm about to go pick her up from work now." He pulled his cell out of his pocket and checked the time. "I'm supposed to be there at seven."

"I see. Well..." The line went silent.

"Hello?"

"I'm here. I tried to call her cell, but she didn't answer." Gladys took a deep breath. "Why are you picking her up from work? Is there something wrong with her car?"

"No. Her car is fine, but is everything okay with you?" Antonio asked concerned by the idle chit chat. That was not Gladys's normal mode of operation. She was usually straight to the point.

"I hope so," she said.

"What do you mean, Gladys? If you have something on your mind, just say it."

"Rhonda and Titus are living in Atlanta. He has been calling around looking for Rhonda. She, apparently, left their child at home alone and now the child is in custody of DHR. He said he has not seen her in over a week."

Antonio's mouth flew wide open in shock. "She left the baby at home and now she is missing? That is awful."

"Yep, to say the least."

Once again, he looked at his cell phone. That time he checked the date. "What is this April fool or something?"

"You know I don't play like that. It's the absolute God's honest truth. I just got off the phone with Titus and he is worried sick about her."

"I hope Rhonda is okay, but this is the last thing we need right now."

"I hesitated about telling Shayla this, but I know how much she cares about Rhonda. Thick or thin, they will always be like sisters."

"Yeah, with Rhonda as a sister who needs enemies?" he said nonchalantly.

"I know, right. If it were me, I wouldn't think twice about her, but Shayla has a soft spot for Rhonda and I respect Shayla."

Antonio rubbed his temples. "Thanks for the heads up. I'll talk to you later."

"Okay. You guys take care."

"Sure thing." Antonio hung up the phone and shook off the inconvenient and intrusive news about Shayla's ex-husband and trifling friend. Gladys definitely left him with a lot on his mind.

He was anxious to spend a romantic evening with his wife. The last thing he wanted to do was talk about the ratchetness of Titus and Rhonda, so he didn't.

An enjoyable evening began with a comedy show that was off the chain. There were laughs shared by all. After the show, they headed to the restaurant.

Once seated, he took Shayla's hands in his. "I want you to be safe on your trip to Baltimore."

"Lemme tell you somethin'. You can call me Fire Marshall Bill, I'm always safe," she joked.

Antonio laughed. "So, now you've got jokes. Don't get comfortable when you travel. There are too many crazy people out there."

"I will be fine. Besides, Lissa will be flying with me and we are rooming together."

"That's good babe. You are always my number one concern. Do you know how much I think about you so much every single day?"

Shayla blushed and her lips puckered. "No, I don't know how much you think about me. I hoped you would tell me."

"From the moment I pull out of the driveway in the morning, all I want to do is rush back home to have these kinds of moments with you."

Her eyes traveled from his chest to his lips, and then she glanced carefully into his eyes. "I may seem caught up in my work a lot, but I feel the same way."

"You are following your dreams and I wouldn't have it any other way. I will continue to fight for nights like this to rekindle our love. I love you, woman."

"I love you, too."

"Some people said we moved too fast when we got married. But, I don't think there is a time limit that tells the heart when love is supposed to become official."

They met when he worked as a pool serviceman years ago. At the time, she was wrapped up in Titus and his affair. He was a college student working part time to help pay for tuition. At first, she didn't entertain the attraction that sparked between them. However, truth be told, she knew from the first moment she laid eyes on him that he was a special man. She just thought he would be special for someone else. She never expected a turn of events would put them on the same page, as lovers. "The heart knows who it loves," she agreed.

Unable to keep her eyes off him, Shayla felt warm all over. She picked up her glass of wine and took a swallow.

"I have loved you ever since we used to hang out at Tanya's apartment. Those long talks and lunch dates helped me get to know your heart," he reminded her.

"Love is a mysterious thing."

"You bet your sweet lips it is. Speaking of lips," he said before licking his sexy, brown lips. "I haven't tasted yours today."

"What are you going to do to change that?" she challenged.

He stood up and walked around the table to stand beside her chair. He helped her up from her seat and kissed her long and hard.

A few guests in the restaurant paid close attention to their heated kiss. Some gave Antonio the thumbs up while others pointed in amusement.

After he broke the kiss, Shayla said, "Mr. Davis, if you kiss me like that one more time, we won't be having dinner tonight."

"That's a thought," he said, eying the door.

She nervously placed a piece of hair behind her ear. "We've already ordered, so let's stay. We can definitely skip dessert though."

"Oh, I'm having dessert. It just won't be served from their kitchen." He winked, and then helped her back into her seat.

"I hope the service is fast, so we can get home early," she said once seated.

Antonio moved his chair close to her and they talked like two lovebirds. Over dinner, Shayla told Antonio about the different things that went on in the office with the new health care regulations.

The nagging thought about Rhonda Wilson being on her appointment book crossed her mind. For the first time since coming into the restaurant, her mood went somber.

"What's wrong?" Antonio asked realizing her sudden mood change.

"Nothing, just thinking about one of my clients at work," she said, which was not entirely a lie. Realizing that thinking about Rhonda was dampening the evening, Shayla changed the subject to a lighter topic. "I am so happy for Gladys. She and Maverick have come a long way. Even though they are waiting to get married, they are so happy," Shayla said as the waitress arrived with their food order.

Antonio shifted in his seat. He knew that eventually he would have to tell Shayla about Gladys' call. Once the food was set up on the table, they dug into the delicious meal. Every few minutes, Antonio admired the beauty of his wife. He winked at her, caressed her hand, or did something to connect with her on an intimate level.

Her radiant glow showed that she was outdone with excitement. Knowing her husband well, she knew the affection he showed in the restaurant was only a preview of the attention he would give her later that night.

"What?" she said in response to him quietly staring at her.

"I want to kiss your lips again," he said as she moved her wine glass from her lips.

"Touché," she said. She leaned in and kissed him again.

Once he broke the kiss, he said, "When we make love tonight, I want it to feel as if it is our last time. I want to take it slow, careful not to repress one savory emotion."

"I like slow," Shayla said, squirming in her chair.

"Release your pinned up frustrations and feelings. Baby, I want you to completely intertwine and unwind with me." His voice was close to her ear, low and sensual.

"Antonio, if you keep talking that way, I don't think I will make it on that plane tomorrow morning."

"You'll be good and ready in the morning but, until your departure, am I wrong for wanting you to experience sensations so strong that every vibration in every nerve ending in your body will be screaming my name by the end of the night?"

Shayla crossed and uncrossed her legs. She took a sip of her wine. "No...no, you are not wrong for that!"

She spoke louder than anticipated. Customers in the restaurant were once again looking in their direction. Shayla was swept away and didn't care who knew it. Her face expressed passion she never had with another being. As far as she was concerned, she hoped to never share that passion with another person again.

"Can you handle it?" he asked as he took a sip of his wine and winked at her.

"Like the little red engine that could, I think I can handle *all* of that."

"If you do, I promise a flowing river of love as you take the ride of your life."

"I like that," she said totally engaged in his sexy war of words.

"I'm going to give you every inch of me. No holding back. Since you've got the best loving on this side of the equator, I won't ask for more. No, that would not be good enough. I will beg for one more eternal dive into your lovely abyss."

"Oh, really?" she flirted, loving when his dirty talk flowed like a poetic river.

"Oh, yes. As we sway to the slow and steady beat of our love, moving fast, eager, and rough, you will understand that my flesh is hungry for you. My body is longing for you. Heated touches will become a source of craving for more heat."

"You poetic beast, you..." Shayla said as she scooted to the edge of her seat and squirmed with excitement. The moisture building between her legs was hot like lava. "Do tell me more."

"I'll bring forth pleasures and extract such a beautiful passion; it will be like a Picasso painting, one in a million. Can you see it, babe?"

"Yes! I see it! I see it!" she screamed. Her eyes drifted off to the sensual place he captured so magically with words.

"Imagine that instead of the colors of a painting being displayed vivid for your eyes to see, deep pants and sultry gazes into each other eyes paints an exquisite picture of ecstasy that sends us to a colorful museum of artistry's pleasures. In this place, the only

27

two people suitable to judge the beauty of this portrait are you and me."

"Nowhere on God's green earth is there another me and you," Shayla said on the verge of a mental orgasm. She was ripe with passion.

"They say tomorrow is never promised, so we have to love like it is the last time. Our last chance is today."

With those sweet words of mental sex dancing through her ears, Shayla called out to the nearest waiter for the check. "Check, please!"

When she awoke for her trip the next morning, she looked and felt like a million bucks. She smiled at Antonio as he helped her pack her bags and briefcase in the car. By six o'clock they headed out.

"Thank you for last night," she said once they were in the car.

"It was great wasn't it, especially when we got home." Antonio said with a devilish grin on his face. "My favorite part was when you did that handstand and…"

"Shhh, Tyler is back there."

They both looked at Tyler sitting on the backseat playing with his electronic game. He was the least bit concerned with what his parents discussed.

Antonio said, "He's in his own world."

"Yeah, I guess so, but he doesn't need to hear anything about mommy's handstands." She tapped Antonio on the arm and laughed.

"I know, but honey you are amazing," he said. Once they turned out of their neighborhood, he decided to tell her about Gladys' call. "I forgot to tell you that Gladys called last night," he said, still waging over whether or not to tell her.

She let out a long yawn. "Really, how is she doing?"

Antonio's voice dropped a few decibels. "She said she is doing well. But, that was not why she called."

Shayla looked at him with a side eye. "Well, why did she call?"

"To let you know Rhonda left her child at home alone last week and no one has seen her since. DHR has custody of the child now and Titus is looking for her."

The correlation between what Antonio said and the fact that Rhonda's name landed on her schedule for the following week was too much. Her eyes doubled in size. He continued, "Can you believe she would leave a five year old at home alone? And to top it off, Gladys said they are living in Atlanta now."

"What did you say?"

"I said she has been gone for over a week and she left her child at home alone."

"No, the part about them living in Atlanta."

"Yeah." His grip tightened on the steering wheel. "She said they live in Atlanta now. All I said was that his weak ass better not come near you!"

"Don't talk that way, Antonio. We can't let their actions change who we are. We have worked too hard to get to where we are today to let those two knock us back down. We are saved, blessed and highly favored."

He sighed and said, "I know, baby." He slowly ran a finger over the softness of her hand. His touch caused her to smile. "It's just that those two are trouble and I have no doubt that they are planning to bring that trouble to our doorstep."

She thought long and hard before saying, "I have to tell you something."

"What?"

Antonio braced himself for her answer. "I'm sure that there is more than one Rhonda Wilson in Atlanta. However, the receptionist got a call from a woman by that name that supposedly has some issues from her past that are in her words, *haunting* her. With what Gladys said and this out of the blue appointment, I bet it is Rhonda."

Antonio looked at Shayla in disbelief. Then, he spoke with absolute authority. "I don't want you to see her. Cancel the appointment."

Shayla put a finger to his lips to calm him. "I'm going to find out if it is her first. Then, I will find out what she wants. Promise that you will let me deal with it and I promise that it will not come to our doorstep."

"Shayla, I'm not about to let them come into our life and start playing games with us. I will bust a cap in both their raggedy asses before that happens." He turned his eyes back to the road.

"Promise me."

"I promise to let you deal with it, unless it becomes more than you can deal with. Then, I will handle it my way and, trust me, you will not like my way."

"Deal. Now, let's spend the rest of this ride in peace. Let's not talk about anyone else but us."

Antonio agreed and placed a kiss on her cheek. Within minutes they were at Lissa's apartment.

The ride to the airport was quiet. Once they arrived, Antonio got out and opened Shayla's door. He helped her out of the car and directly into his arms.

"I'm going to miss you," he said, kissing her hard on the lips.

"You know you two should get a room," Lissa teased before getting out of the car to get her bags.

"I'll call you as soon as I touch down," she said to him before getting her bags out of the car, as well.

"I'll be waiting." Antonio helped Shayla carry her bags to the front desk. She checked in for her flight and headed to the carry-on bag check area. Once there, her text message alarm rang.

Beautiful Lady, I just wanna say have a safe trip. You know I struggle when you are gone and after last night it's going to be hard not seeing you for the next few days. Be careful and get back home safe. I love you :)

She smiled wishing she could turn around, go home and spend the rest of the morning in between her warm sheets, with her husband.

Secrets of a Kept Woman 2 | Shani Greene-Dowdell

Chapter 4

Lissa

Lissa had a simple formula to charming people. First she warmed them up and injected a full dose of light-hearted humor mixed with a teaspoon of business savvy. Then, she closed the deal with a riveting offer that couldn't be refused.

Her down-to-earth and jokingly, cunning approach to relationships was a complete contrast to her title of Chief Operations Officer of Naytek Media Groups, one of the most cut-throat positions in the company. She had been at the helm of the enterprise for four years strong.

The trip to Baltimore was supposed to be about business, but Lissa had every intention to sneak in a little pleasure, as well. If she played her cards right, a particular unsuspecting businessman would have her bells ringing like a Wall Street trade room by the end of

33

the night. *I'm not asking for a lifetime, just one night on the nightstand.* She laughed at her naughty thought as she exited the airport with her luggage in tow.

After arriving at the hotel, she checked in and got dressed for the first event of the day. The Work Your Business Convention was a lively event packed with movers and shakers from all over the United States who met up for the best inspirational speaking, business tips, and networking in the country.

After she stepped into the auditorium, it didn't take long before she spotted Seth Baker. A go getter in his own right, he was a trendsetter who happened to be filthy rich. She did everything in her power to get closer than close, including sitting in the front row wearing a hot black mini skirt that exposed her perfect size six brown legs. No man in his right, heterosexual mind would overlook her thighs in that skirt.

From the looks that he gave her as he spoke so eloquently to the audience, he'd love the opportunity to get to know her better or at least the opportunity to get to know what was under her skirt better.

She did her research before she left Atlanta and found that he was a Harvard Law School graduate who took an interest in entertainment law. He had an eye for investments, so he positioned himself as a successful entertainment investor. He invested in some of the most popular world tours of both Christian and pop artists. He was an accomplished businessman who, by all intents and purposes, was fine, intelligent, powerful, and available.

On first sight, he invoked thoughts of wedding bouquets, bridal showers, and wedding arrangements including colors, dresses, catering, and of course a long honeymoon.

Alongside Reverend Drakes, Seth offered a dynamic speech about going after what you want in life. Lissa's favorite line from his speech had been, 'The first step to happiness is pursuit.'

Instead of allowing those words to motivate her to move her life and company to higher heights of happiness and success. She took the message to mean that the Hennessey-colored molten, honey brother standing at the podium was happiness, for which that weekend, she would be in pursuit. She thought carefully of a way to engage him.

I guess I could strike up a conversation about his seminar. "Nah, that's probably what half of the women here plan to do," she said under her breath, looking around to notice several women gawking over him with dreamy eyes. Whatever she would say to him would be bold, confident, and levels above those poor little women.

I'll ask him about a nightcap at his hotel – straight to the point, no chaser. Yeah, I like that, she thought. She decided to let small talk lead to asking if she could spend the night in his hotel room. As soon as the thought crossed her mind, she knew she was wrong, possibly even dead wrong. However, she reasoned that sometimes a woman had to follow her body's needs and at that moment her body was in need of Seth Baker.

35

At the close of his seminar, she glanced at Shayla who had been taking tons of notes. "I will be right back. I'm going to check this speaker out and see if he can give me a one-on-one motivational session tonight." Lissa was up out of her seat before Shayla could object.

Shayla pulled Lissa's jacket and warned, "He looks like a playa with a history of getting conference booty, so be careful."

"I got this," were Lissa's only words before she waded through the crowd. It didn't take long before she was standing face-to-face with him. Getting a full view of his handsome face, she marveled over his smooth skin that held the texture of whipped butter mixed with chocolate.

His scent was heavenly. His lips began to move, but she could barely hear the words coming out of his mouth.

"Thanks for joining the workshop," he said extending his hand for a shake.

She extended her freshly manicured hand for a shake. With the handshake, she verified that there was no ring on his finger. That detail made the nicely dressed, well spoken man move into the looking-like-a million-bucks-dipped-in-gold category.

She managed to say, "I really enjoyed your seminar. Your ideas for working your business are genius! It was very inspirational and game changing. How long have you been speaking at the Work Your Business Convention?" she asked.

"Well, Lissa," he said as if they were old friends. "It is pronounced Lissa McDaniels correct?"

"That's right."

"This is my second year speaking, but I have been Vice President of this conference since it started ten years ago. I was a part of the team that founded it." He cradled the palm of her hand so that it fit nicely within his, holding her hand long enough for it to be established that he didn't want the innocence of their contact to end with small talk.

The mahogany wood scented cologne did not help the chills that ran up and down her entire body. Struggling to keep her infatuation under control, she knew beyond a shadow of a doubt that their chemistry was strong. He was a perfect match.

Dang girl, calm down, she told herself. *You just met the man, so perfect match is a bit much.*

She crooked her neck to one side, raised an eyebrow and ran her tongue over her lips before saying, "Thousands of people attend this mega conference annually and you know me by name? How does that happen?" A warm smile spread across her face.

"I make it my business to know every person of importance," Seth said, and then let out a light chuckle.

Her eyes fluttered as her cheeks became flushed. "So, you think I'm important, huh?"

His look was intense as he continued to hold her hand in his. He explained, "Well, usually you send someone from the middle management team to represent.. I am glad that you are here, but make no mistake about it, we always lay out the red carpet for Naytek with front row seating and I make it my business to know their names. However, when I heard you were going to be here in the flesh, I added a few extra perks, including access to private sessions." The devilish fire burning in his eyes as he said private sessions overshadowed the bright and huge innocent smile on his face.

She was proud to work for such a respected company. "I guess you have a point there. Naytek does run the electronic medical record software industry. I'm sure you have done business with one of our many reps at one point or another."

"Sure have," he said in agreement.

"So, you are the man in charge of this conference? Impressive," Lissa said and giggled coyly. They shared an awkward moment of silence, and then she added, "It is so nice to meet you. I'm putting some of your strategies to use at Naytek as soon as I get back Monday." She sort of extended the truth. The main thing she learned was that she wanted some Seth Baker in her life.

There was another second or two of awkward silence that Seth broke. "So, how was your flight from Atlanta?"

"It was smooth. No turbulence, no turbans, and the terror alert status was low; therefore, all was well in the friendly skies." She giggled, giving him full view of her pearly white teeth.

Before he could respond, another attendee walked over and tapped him on the shoulder. Lissa observed him tentatively as he greeted the person. She committed as many details about him as she could to memory. If it was her last chance to soak him all in, her sponge would be full. Once he returned his attention to her, he said, "Sorry about that. When you are the man in charge, people are always walking up with questions."

"Understood." She gauged the fact that her hand was *still* cradled in his, and decided to extend an offer. "So, ah... Seth what exactly are you doing after you leave the event this evening?"

"I don't really have any..." She moved a little closer to him and his words caught in his throat. With a gulp of air he finished his sentence. "...plans."

She whispered in his ear, allowing her hot breath to drive her point home. "I was thinking it would be nice if you would give me one of your private sessions where we can go over some of the penetrating thoughts from your seminar."

He raised his left eyebrow and looked at her as if she'd given him the offer of a lifetime. "Since you put it like that, I'm open for discussion."

Chapter 5

Lissa

"Last night was beautiful, Seth," Lissa said, entangled in his hotel bed covers. After leaving the convention, they had dinner, a few drinks, and caught a movie premiere. Then, they went back to his suite for what was supposed to be a simple nightcap but ended up being the longest nightcap filled with sparks and flames that lasted well into the mid-morning hours.

"I agree. Spike's new movie was good," his baritone voice filled the room like music to her ears.

"It was a good movie." She rolled her eyes away from him. "But, was that the only part about last night that you thought was good?"

As she pouted, he stole a kiss from her lips and said, "Not exactly the only part." He kissed her neck, chest, and placed tender kisses on her breasts.

"You'd better stop. This is starting to feel too good to be a one-night stand," she said as he kissed her in places that had not been kissed in years before that night.

He kissed her forehead and said, "I liked that part." He kissed her nose. "And that part." He kissed her each cheek. "And this part." He kissed behind each ear. "And especially these parts." He kissed her neck. "And this part." He kissed the center of her chest. "And this part." He kissed each breast. "I'm in love with these parts." He kissed her stomach. "And this part is close to the best part."

With every kiss, she let out a soft moan. "I could get used to this," she said when he kissed her stomach.

"I want you to get used to this," he stated matter-of-factly. He looked into her eyes before planting more kisses on her skin. "Because I will be coming back for more."

The thought of him coming back for more was cute. However, she was a realist. She knew a long distance relationship that began with screwing on the first night of a business conference was not exactly the beginning of a fairytale. Though her mind resisted, she relaxed and allowed her body to enjoy the pleasures of the moment.

"You can't just do a girl like this first thing in the morning! You are so wrong," she said when he kissed between her thighs.

He climbed on top of her and looked at her eye to eye. "Do you want me to stop?"

"Of course not. Now, kiss my lips again. They miss you."

He obliged, placing the most tender and loving kiss on her lips. The kiss was passionate, intimate, and different. It caught her off guard. She ended the kiss quickly and looked away from him.

"Is everything okay?" he asked.

"Yeah, I'm good. It's just…" She laid still for a few minutes, trying to think of ways to finish her sentence. Instead, she kissed his neck. "It's just that I want to feel you."

"Not as bad as I want to feel you again," he said and pulled her close. For the next hour, he aimed to please as he eagerly explored the depth of her womanhood.

A few hours later, she was lying in his arms thinking about how much she didn't want their time together to end. However, she was determined not to rush things. She had enough business smarts to know that every deal that came as easy and sweet as a night with Seth Baker had the potential to turn sour just as quickly as it was sweet.

Chapter 6

Tom

Upon finding out she was leaving town, he hacked into her office computer, found the hotel she was staying in and followed her to Baltimore. Once there, he made the proper arrangements, so he would know the happenings inside her hotel room at all times. Disguised as an older gentleman, he arrived to the hotel before they got there .Sitting in the lobby with a newspaper covering his face, he watched them check in and listened closely as the hotel clerk gave their room assignment.

Once the two unsuspecting ladies walked away, he walked over to the clerk and checked in. "Yes, I'd like to check in for two days."

"Sure, can I see your identification?" the bubbly young woman asked. He slid his ID and credit card across the counter. The woman took the cards and scanned them. "Have you ever rented a room at the Hilton?" she asked.

"No, but I would like my room to be on the second floor, preferably room number 209," Tom said as the hotel clerk keyed his information into the system. "It overlooks the city," he said when she gave him a strange look.

"Let me check and see if we have that room available," she said. A few seconds later, she confirmed, "You are in luck! Room 209 is available."

She handed him the key card and then said, "Enjoy your stay, Mr. Bradley."

"Thank you," he said as he walked toward the elevator.

As soon as the ladies left for the conference, he waited in the hall for a maid. After about fifteen minutes, he was in luck.

"Ma'am, I must have left my key in the room. Will you let me back in my room?" he asked a tall, slender black woman wearing a Hilton uniform.

"Sure." She kindly opened Shayla's room door and allowed him into the ladies room.

"Thank you so much. I can be so forgetful." He entered the room and within ten minutes the hidden camera was set up. He exited the room.

Later that evening, Tom was sitting on his bed when he saw Shayla's room door open. "Thank the heavens that bitch found something else to do, besides ruining my evening," he said of Lissa when Shayla arrived back to her room alone.

46

Too much time had passed since he last laid eyes on her and, before his eyes would be satisfied enough to close, her beautiful essence had to float across his pupils.

Over the course of a year, Tom had become addicted to seeing her. He couldn't live without the thought of her naked body being close to him. That day was no different. He had to see her. Without Lissa around, he could spend uninterrupted moments watching Shayla's every move.

After being secluded in his room all day waiting for her to return from the conference, he was awestruck when she walked across her room. Standing in the middle of his suite, he stalked the surveillance stream, waiting for her to come out of the bathroom.

When she walked out and into her suite naked, the stalker's dream had come true. He immediately felt connected to her as if their bodies were one. Her body looked like a silken rose as she glided across the floor toward the dresser drawer. He laid down on the bed mesmerized at the thought of her beauty. Arousal was a consequence.

"The first thing she will do is apply a coat of Moroccan oil to her hair," he said, familiar with her nightly routine.

Shayla applied Moroccan oil to her hair and then picked up her lotion bottle to moisten her skin.

"After applying a coat of lotion, she will then place a small amount of perfume on the nape of her neck. Then, she will put on her pajamas. I wonder what she will wear tonight," he said as he sat in wonder of Shayla's movements.

She applied a dab of her favorite perfume to nape of her neck, reached into the drawer, and took out a white silk gown.

"She will slip the gown on slowly, being careful not to mess up her hair," Tom said as he began to touch himself down low. "She hates to mess up her hair."

Shayla slipped on the white, silk gown slowly and careful, not wanting to rearrange her hair. When the gown was on, she picked up her brush and brushed each hair back into place.

He imagined the lovely fragrance she wore penetrating the hotel walls. He imagined how lovely she smelt each night when she went to bed. He loved everything about her. The way she walked. The way she stood in her mirror to admire her beautiful reflection. The way she looked over her shoulder to smile at him once she was satisfied with her bedtime preparations.

"Aw, look at her. She wants to be with me as much as I want to be with her," he said with adoration, but then worry lines began to appear on his forehead when she took a deep breath and sighed. "My baby is exhausted. Go to sleep my sweet baby. Get some rest."

He was disappointed when, instead of sleeping as he urged, she picked up the telephone and slid underneath the covers. Tom grimaced, thinking about who was on the other end of the call.

"I wish she would not interrupt our precious time together by calling him." The same way he knew her routine for nightly grooming, he knew she would make a call to her husband.

"Hello, babe," she said. A big smile spread across her face as she spoke to Antonio.

Tom pretended she was talking to him and answered, "Hi, babe. Please, come over to my suite tonight." His single wish was that he was the person on the other end of her call. He felt if she would listen to him, he would tell her how much he loved her. He would promise to treat her better than ever before.

"Really? How much do you miss me?" she said, interrupting his thoughts.

The realization of how happy she was to talk to the lucky man on the other end of her phone hit Tom hard.

"Oh, you just don't know how much I miss you, Mr. Davis. You do not understand the things I would do to you if I was home now," she said holding the cell phone close to her ear.

The seductive look on her face made Tom expressionless. "Home?" he questioned. The loneliness of his desperate hotel room with his surveillance setup was palpable. He didn't have the pleasure of calling any particular place home and had not in years.

"Don't you even try to get anything started on this phone," she said, bringing his attention back to the surveillance stream. "I'm going to take care of you when I see you tomorrow night." She touched her breast as if she desired to be touched in that spot.

Tom imagined that touch had come from him.

"I just called to give you a tele-kiss good night," she said blowing a kiss into the phone.

The kiss traveled through the air and Tom caught it and placed it on his lips.

"And kiss my baby for me," she said before ending the call.

Before she placed the phone on the nightstand, Tom's hand traveled inside his pants. Taking note to the raging desire burning inside of him, he contemplated going ahead with his plan for an ultimate reunion with her right then, but it was too soon. Their reunion had to be well planned out.

Am I wrong for falling in love with her? The question tugged at him until he noticed she had gotten out of bed to apply more oil to her legs. One look at the beautiful woman on the screen and he knew he was not wrong for loving her. Who wouldn't love a woman who loved herself the way Shayla did?

Once she applied the oil that was anything but the oil of Christ to her legs, she crawled into the bed and to Tom's surprise, looked at the camera and deeply into his eyes. She writhed her sensual body about the bed so much that Tom reached out to touch her.

After a few minutes of struggling with whether to walk over to her room and proclaim his love for her or to wait patiently, he opened his door and walked out into the hall.

"No, it is too soon," an inner voice spoke to him.

Willing himself back into his hotel, he closed the door and fixed his eyes back on the surveillance stream. Her fingers touched every part of her body. He imagined she was thinking of him as she pleasured herself, until she said the words that kicked his soul and shattered it into a thousand pieces.

"Oh, I miss you, Mr. Antonio Davis!" She looked at her husband's picture on her cell phone, and then dozed off to sleep.

Once she was asleep, Tom imagined making the sweetest love to her, so sweet that the only name she would remember was his.

Chapter 7

Lissa

Lissa boarded the plane Sunday evening, floating on air. "Hey, friend!" she said to Shayla in a high-pitched greeting.

On the other hand, Shayla was one hundred and thirty degrees hot. "Don't 'hey friend me' after you call and ask me to lug your luggage from the hotel because you decided to shack up with Mr. Baker, the event planner, for the entire weekend."

"First of all, he is not an event planner. He is a keynote speaker and conference leader. Second of all, we didn't shack up."

"If you didn't shack up, what do you call it?"

"We opened a new business deal and spent time exploring the different options."

"More like exploring the different positions," Shayla said watching her friend blush. "I called your phone twenty times last night and you didn't answer."

Lissa huffed and sat down in her seat by the window. She buckled her seatbelt and looked out of the window in deep thought. "I'm sorry, Shayla. I don't know what I've gotten myself into. When I was with him, I didn't think of anything else but him. It was like I was incapable of focusing on anything else. That is how I know the struggle is about to get real."

"Cry me a river," Shayla said rolling her eyes away from her lust-sick friend.

"A man like Seth Baker gets all in your pores. It is going to be hard to go back to Atlanta and not think about him." She paused, looking at Shayla who was busy trying to arrange her carry-on bag in the overhead compartment. "It's obvious that you have no sympathy for my pain."

"I'm just glad to know that instead of some serial killer kidnapping and throwing you into the Patapsco River, you're okay because Mr. Baker was getting into your pores."

"Ugh! You read too much news and worry too much, Shayla. Sometimes you have to relax and enjoy life."

As Shayla rammed her oversized bag into the small compartment, another passenger walked over to help. "Ma'am, let me get that for you," the raspy voiced male said.

Shayla turned to see an elderly, brown-skinned man with a large hat and dark glasses assisting her.

"No. I'll get it," she said, but was too late.

He took the bag out of her hand and gently placed it into an empty space above Shayla's seat. "I wouldn't dare allow you to do that, little mama," he said.

Shayla tilted her head to the side and looked at the man long and hard. "What did you say?"

I said, "I got it in there for you. Good day, lady," he said tilting his hat before turning to walk away.

"Thanks," she said, shaking the instinct that the man reminded her of someone she knew.

"It was nice of that frail old man to help you, especially when some young men of today's society won't lift a finger to help a woman move something heavy, much less assist with a carry-on bag," Lissa said as they watched the gentleman go to his seat at the back of the plane.

"Yeah," Shayla agreed, but there was something about the man and the way he said 'little mama' reminded her of a person in her past.

Lissa said, "I guess chivalry ain't dead, huh? The old dudes are still trying to hold it down for the whole male species."

Shayla smiled and nodded her head in agreement. "I'm still mad at you, so don't change the subject. The only way I am going to become un-mad at you is if you give me all of the juicy details!"

Lissa waved her hand and shook her head. "Uh uh. A real lady never tells."

Shayla shook her head and said, "Chile, there is nothing lady like about running off like you did last night."

"Look, I told you I'm so sorry for not answering my phone. I'm not going to keep taking this verbal abuse from you. You are killing my Seth high."

"Lissa, you had me worried sick when I woke up and saw that you were not back in the room this morning. A lot of things can happen to a young, pretty lady in a strange city. Bad things. I'm a psychiatrist, so I know the horrors in some people's minds. You could have at least called me to let me know that you were okay. Do I need to give you a few free therapy sessions to help you get your mind right?"

"I can't say just yet, but after last night, I believe I will be going through withdrawals soon. A therapy session might be in order."

Shayla digressed. "Well, it must have been some good-good loving, because you are freaking glowing, not to mention smiling like you just hit the multistate mega millions lottery."

"It was what it was." Lissa shivered as if she was reliving a sweet moment from her encounter. "Let's just say what happens in Baltimore, will hopefully happen again in Atlanta."

Shayla gave her a high five and said, "Well, if it was that damn good, I will give you a pass this one time. Next time, answer your phone!"

On that note, they both prepared for the flight back home. The flight attendant announced over the intercom the rundown of rules, precautions for takeoff, and emergencies. Within minutes of takeoff, both ladies had drifted fast asleep.

Chapter 8

Lissa

Lissa struggled not to read too much between the lines. She didn't want to put stock into the *just because* text messages Seth sent every hour since she arrived home. However, the flowers waiting on her desk Monday morning when she got to work had her smiling from ear to ear. "Seth, you are so sweet," she said when she called to thank him.

"Do you like them?"

"Do I? They are beautiful." She picked up the bouquet and smelled each rose one by one. Every detail about his essence was locked in her memories and she had thrown away the key. Standing there smelling the bouquet of roses and hearing his voice on the other end of the phone, she imagined seeing him again.

"I'm glad you like them. A beautiful woman like you deserves to smell a bouquet of roses on Monday mornings."

The receptionist buzzed her line, announcing the appointment Lissa had been preparing for. "Mrs. McDaniels, your ten o'clock appointment is here."

"Give me a minute, and then send her in," Lissa told her assistant.

"Duty calls."

"Ah, I heard her," he said disappointed about the inopportune time of the assistant's announcement.

"Seth, honey, thank you for the flowers."

"You are more than welcome."

Lissa took a deep breath and placed the bouquet on top of her bookshelf. "I will call you later?"

"Please do. I'll be off around five."

She smiled. "It's a phone date."

Lissa ended the call and buzzed her assistant. "Send her in."

She reached into the file cabinet beside her desk to get the paperwork for Jennifer Sinclair-Baker, a local software consultant she hired to improve the software integration process at Naytek.

"Good morning, Mrs. Sinclair-Baker. Come in and have a seat." Lissa pointed to the empty chair in front of her desk and Mrs. Sinclair-Baker sat down.

Taking time to slowly look around at the different fixtures in the office, the woman nodded her head and extended her hand for a shake. "Yes, Miss. McDaniels, nice to meet you. Or is it Mrs.?"

Lissa laughed as she extended her hand, as well, for a quick shake. "It's just Miss, but I'm actively working on changing that."

"That project is bigger than the one I am here to help with; I'm sure of it. The way men are these days. You'll be lucky to find a half decent, half straight man that doesn't wear skinny legged jeans or too baggy jeans. One who actually believes that he should have to work for a living," she said with her voice dripping sarcasm.

They shared an awkward moment as Mrs. Sinclair-Baker shifted in her seat.

"Okay, let's get down to business." Lissa opened the yellow folder on her desk. Scanning through the pages, she said, "Well, let's see, Mrs. Sinclair-Baker..."

"Oh, please, call me Jennifer."

"Okay, Jennifer, it looks as if we have our work cut out for us. Getting the MasterLine documentation software up to snuff before January is going to be a challenge, to say the least. Have you had a chance to look the files over that I emailed you on Friday?"

"Yes, I did and I actually have an idea for a direction we should go."

"Oh really? What do you have in mind to get us started?"

"First, I want you to understand that the best documentation software consultant in the United States is sitting in front of you. So, when I say I have an idea for the direction we should go, please know that I have a plan from start to the finish. This project will be done in time to do Christmas shopping and sip champagne as we welcome the New Year in with our families, please believe me."

Though Lissa liked the sound of that, she was skeptical. "I only work with the best. That is why you are here. So as a game plan, what do you say about getting started on the glitch in retrieving the documents after reboot?"

"That's the plan, but as a general rule I start at the finish line," Jennifer said as she clapped her hands together and pulled out her laptop.

After two hours of hashing out details and writing out plans to get the documentation project moving forward, Lissa closed out their meeting.

"Wow! You were right. Working at this pace, we'll be done in no time. I'll get my to-do list worked out by the close of business tomorrow, and then we will take the plan to the implementation team for their input."

"That sounds great, since we are working on a tight deadline," Jennifer replied.

"I try to do everything with urgency whether it is on time or late," she said. She then thought of how she expertly and urgently ravished Seth Baker.

"I will check back with you on Monday to see how things are progressing," Jennifer said pulling her out of her thoughts.

"Great! I'll have an update for you then."

Once Jennifer left the office, Lissa decided to take the rest of the afternoon off. Before leaving, she composed an email to her secretary listing things that she would like done before the next morning. She also drafted an email to the implementation team with a summary of the plan from her meeting with Jennifer. Just as she was about to walk out of her office, her direct line rang. Direct calls were not screened by her secretary and usually were important. She put her purse down and sprinted to the phone.

"Hello, Lissa McDaniels, the problem solver speaking!"

"I have a few problems for you to solve."

"Seth?"

"I don't know what it is about you, but you have been on my mind since we talked this morning."

"Really?"

"Yes, really. Did you check your text messages?"

"I have been in a meeting for the past two hours, so I have not even looked at my phone."

"Well, I basically said that I missed my honey-flavored temptress from Atlanta. I think I'll have to see you really soon."

Lissa wrapped the phone cord around her fingers and asked, "Is that what men are calling us now, temptresses?"

"No, that's what I'm calling you."

"Well, I don't know if I like that name yet," she said lowly.

"Open your office door and let's see if I can help change your mind about it."

"My office door?" Lissa walked to the door and as sure as she had breath in her body, he stood in the doorway with yet another bouquet of flowers in his hand.

"My God Seth! What are you doing here? I didn't expect you to come to town this soon."

"You will learn to expect the unexpected with me," he said handing her the flowers. "Didn't I tell you when you were in Baltimore?"

"Tell me what?" she asked taking the flowers from his hands.

He walked into her office and made himself comfortable on the sofa. "That I have a second home here in Atlanta."

"*You* have a house in Atlanta?"

"Atlanta is the hub of black business and events. It's only natural that I have a house here. I do a lot of business in both places."

"That...is...interesting," she said, seduction dripping from each word. She imagined all of the wondrous things she would do to him while he was at his home away from home in Atlanta. "How long are you going to be in town? We have to get together and do something while you are here."

"How about now?"

Lissa raised an eyebrow. "Now? Of course, now is perfect!" she said to the mound of chocolate sitting on her office sofa. She was exhausted from the weekend and knew the following workday was going to be hectic with the integration project. All good instincts told her that she should go home and rest. However, an intriguing evening with Seth trumped all responsible thoughts.

When he placed a long and sweet kiss on her lips, she knew it would be a long night. They walked out of her office hand-in-hand.

Chapter 9

Jennifer

"What are you doing here?" Jennifer said to her husband when he strolled in shortly after midnight.

She sat up straight on the living room sofa startled by the unusual intrusion and interruption of their marital routine. Sleeping alone on the sofa was a habit. She loathed their immaculate bed with comfortable, oversized pillow top mattresses, and the finest silk sheets and bedspread that money could buy. Those things reminded her of what she did not have. Someone to share the bed with.

For the moment, he ignored her question, turned on a lamp and stood quiet. He didn't have to answer her question with words. She recognized the look on his face. He missed her. She smiled, realizing he needed her as much as she needed him. He'd missed her enough to surprise her with his midnight presence.

Years ago, they traded a steamy, romantic marriage for high maintenance careers that separated them by hundreds of miles. Their current lifestyle included upkeep of two houses in two separate cities. With each passing day, it became harder for her to remember what passion felt like.

He removed his jacket and placed it on the arm of the sofa. "I live here," he finally answered her question.

She smiled through her pain. "It's a pleasant surprise that you remembered you live here. I thought you forgot the address," she said. Her body was stoic. Her voice devoid of emotion.

He removed his pants as he responded. "I missed you and wanted to see you, so I caught a late flight and I'm here." He continued to undress, slowly removing every article of clothing.

"Is that right?" she questioned, not surprised by his actions. It was typical behavior for him. Surprise entry. Straight to the point. No chaser. Seduce. Knock her off her feet. Leave her with his name tattooed on every inch of her body. Then, back to work in separate cities with few phone calls and little attachment.

"Damn right," he affirmed. "I want my wife."

"Now, you want me."

"I always want you and miss you."

"How much have you missed me?" she asked watching him undress and cross the room to join her on the sofa. Anticipation was vivid with every step he took. She wished she could suppress her feelings, but there was no doubt in her mind that she missed and wanted him too.

"This much," he said widening his arms for a hug.

"Is that all?"

"Okay, it was this much," he said stretching his arms as wide as they would stretch. "Have you missed me?"

Her right hand touched his chest pushing him away. "I don't think you would understand how much, if I told you."

"That's why I'm here tonight. Talking to you on the phone is one thing, but you looking me in the eyes and telling me how my favorite girl in the world is doing is priceless."

"I've been good," she lied, determined not to kill the moment.

"Good." He accepted her response with a touch on her chin.

"It's just that..." she paused, unsure if she wanted to interrupt the fanciful moment with reality.

He pulled her close. "Whatever it is, you know you can talk to me."

Her eyes traveled away from his until she was looking at the floor. She knew he could read her like a book so, judging by her actions, the cat was already out of the bag.

"Every time I call your phone you are either busy or not answering at all. And, this weekend, it just went to voicemail the entire weekend. I could have been in a car wreck or something and you did not answer."

"Babe, I turned my phone off because of everything that goes on at the conference and didn't turn it back on. I'm sorry."

"I'm just going to be real and ask you what I am thinking. Are you having an affair?"

"What?" His hand fell from her face in defeat. "No. I don't understand why we always have to have this conversation, either."

"The thought keeps crossing my mind, so I had to ask. I hope you are being honest with me."

"I am being honest. After all, I asked you to come to the conference, but you had other plans. If you were so worried about me having an affair, you would have been there."

"Last weekend was my mother's birthday. You know how important my mother's birthdays are to me."

"I know they are. The only reason I brought it up is because you are accusing me of having an affair. There is no woman in this world that could compare to you, Jennie. I love you."

"Well, if you know that it bothers me when you don't answer my calls, why do you ignore my calls?"

"I'm not ignoring you. I said I turned the phone off because of the business I had to handle this weekend. When I am at work, I am at work." He pulled her close for a hug. "But, if it bothers you that much, I will keep my ringer on from now on."

Typical. His answer was typical. She pulled away from him and walked away, putting distance between them, so she could break the spell only he was able to put on her.

"Aw, come on Jennifer. I would never neglect my special lady," he added. Walking to stand beside her, he tilted her head toward him, so she would look at him.

"You may not be neglecting your special lady, but you are neglecting your wife," she said and turned her head away again.

With an exasperated sigh, he said, "You are special to me and...my wife."

Jennifer began pacing the room. "I don't have a need to be special. I just want you to recognize that I'm worth a phone call."

"Even if I'm in the middle of a million dollar deal, I will make it a priority to answer your calls from now on," he said as he walked toward the kitchen.

"That's the least you can do."

"Look, I'm only here for a short time. Do you want to argue the entire time or do you want to enjoy the time that we have together?"

Jennifer shook her head. Of course, she wanted to say, I want to argue until you understand that I am your wife and that I am top priority. She wanted to tell him that he needed to make it a point that they spend every weekend together when he was not working. She wanted to say that the long distance thing was not working and that either she was moving to Baltimore or he was moving to Atlanta within the month. She wanted to say so many things, but it had been one full month since she felt his warm touch, seven hundred and twenty hours to be exact.

Who was she kidding? It was true that she didn't get to see her husband often. It was also true that she missed him like crazy. Turning on her heels, she slowly walked into the kitchen. Once she stood directly in front of him, she wrapped her arms around him and met his lips with a kiss. As chills traveled up her spine, somewhere deep inside of her soul, she hated the fact that she gave in.

Her hands traveled all over his chest, neck, and head as she kissed him. "Mmmm, I love you so much, Seth," she said looking into his sexy brown eyes.

He pulled her close. "I love you more, Jennie."

Her long pink gown revealed the silhouette of her thickness in the moonlit room. It didn't take long before they were back in the living room with her pajamas sprawled out on the floor besides his clothing.

Memories of the day he shed tears of joy at the altar, the first time he touched the inside of her soul, and the day they purchased their first home flooded her mind. They had history.

"Babe, I'm sorry..." he started to say before she touched his mouth to quiet him. Yet, he kissed her fingers and spoke, "...for making you upset. I'm so sorry."

He helped her onto the sofa and positioned himself on top of her.

"I forgive you," she said as her heart filled with matrimonial love.

As he entered her taut body, he held her tight. "You feel so good, Jennie," he said after releasing a throaty moan.

Savoring every thrust, she whimpered beneath him. "I don't want you to ever leave again," she said as he caressed the skin of her back.

As he journeyed deep into her core, he said, "I don't want to ever leave."

"Don't…"

"We won't have to live apart much longer," he promised looking into her eyes.

"Oh, Seth!" she said holding him tight, slowly grinding her pelvis against his.

"Jennie!" His strokes became urgent and needy. "I love you so much!"

"Not as much as I love you," she said between kisses to his neck, face, chest, fingers.

"Prove it." He turned over to lie on his back and pulled her on top of him and she spent the rest of the night proving her love to her husband with every ounce of energy in her body.

Chapter 10

Jennifer

The next morning, Seth was out of bed at the crack of dawn. In the kitchen, he prepared a big breakfast. When Jennifer walked in the kitchen, a curious look was on her face. She looked in the kitchen closet and cabinets as if she was confused.

"Either someone has kidnapped my husband and replaced him with a cooking robot or I have walked into the wrong kitchen."

He turned around from the stove and smiled at her. "Good morning, my Queen."

"Good morning." She leaned against the wall with her arms crossed. "What are you doing with those pots and pans?"

"What does it look like? I'm cooking breakfast for my wife. I wanted to do breakfast in bed, but you're up now, so we'll have breakfast in here."

Jennifer walked over to the stove and stood beside Seth. She touched his forehead with her right hand. "Are you feeling well?"

"I'm fine."

"I have never known you to get up and cook breakfast. Are you sure there is nothing wrong with you?"

He said firmly, "There is nothing wrong with me. Doing this for you is more about what is right with me, I would think."

On that note, she sat down at the table and prepared to enjoy her meal. "Go for what you know, babe."

"I guess living alone has changed me. I have to eat, so I'm getting used to cooking my own breakfast. I found some good recipes on YouTube, so let me share my culinary skills with you."

"I don't know whether to like the fact that you are cooking for yourself or not. I understand that we are working on our careers, but hate that we live separate. I want to be there to cook your meals and have nights like last night."

He looked back at her. "Last night was great, huh?"

"Fabulous! I don't know how much longer I'll be able to stay in Atlanta without you. You make it hard on a woman," she said as she put one leg up on the chair to get comfortable.

"Things will work out soon." He walked to the table and put eggs on both plates. There was sliced fruit and grits already on the table in covered bowls.

"Honey, this feast you prepared looks delicious."

She watched him go to the coffee maker and brew a pot of coffee. She would have offered to help if he didn't look so overwhelmingly sexy working in the kitchen. Every move he took made her want him more. Times like that made all of their sacrifices worth it.

Chapter 11

Shayla

When Shayla returned to do hospital rounds Monday morning, the first person she had to deal with was Ms. Morris. The woman had another meltdown about her disability check over the weekend. She also had two more patients admitted due to an overdose and a nervous breakdown. By the time Wednesday rolled around, she was completely exhausted with paperwork and clients. Agitating things further was the fact that Rhonda Wilson was still on her schedule for one o'clock.

"Who is going to counsel the counselor?" she asked softly as she stepped into her office thinking about her hectic week. A part of her didn't want to add Rhonda's drama into her case mix. The other part of her wanted to find out what was going on. She also wanted her old friend to see that she was doing just fine without her.

Actually, she wanted her to eat her husband-stealing heart out.

"Mrs. Davis, your one o'clock is here. The receptionist said as soon as the clock struck one. It was apparent by her unprecedented punctual arrival that whatever she wanted to talk about was serious. The Rhonda she remembered was never on time.

"Send her in," she said and took a deep breath. Within seconds of Rhonda walking into the room, Shayla's mouth flew wide open. She fought back the rush of tears threatening to burst from her eyes.

Rhonda was emaciated, only a fraction of the woman she once was. Her eyes were sunken. Her facial bones poked through her skin. Shayla sat in shock unable to move or speak.

"Hi Shayla." Rhonda said as if she could barely get the words through her raspy throat.

Upon hearing her friend's voice, Shayla rushed across the floor and hugged her. "Rhonda! Are you...are you okay?" When Rhonda didn't respond, she gestured for her to take a seat. "Here, have a seat."

After a period of awkward silence, Shayla walked back around to her seat at her desk.

"As you can see, I'm not okay. That is why I needed to talk to you," Rhonda said.

"What is it? Is everything okay with Titus?" At this point, the fact that Titus was her ex-husband did not matter. All she cared about was her friend's wellbeing.

"We're fine," Rhonda said in a defensive tone.

"Oh...okay. Well, what brings you to my office?" Shayla asked as she snapped back to the reality of their relationship.

"After our friendship went to shit, I didn't know what to do with myself."

"That's understandable," Shayla said.

Rhonda rocked back and forth in her seat. "I...I don't have anyone else to talk to."

"Are you sure you want to talk to me?"

"Yes."

"Why is that?"

Rhonda looked firmly into her face and said, "Because, I know that you actually care."

"I guess, when all else fails, you can depend on ole trusty, dusty Shayla to care. She's always there for everyone, but Rhonda who was there for me?" She asked, not sure where her resentful words came from.

"Listen to me," Rhonda pleaded. "I spent all of my life as a woman in search of love. Even though I didn't want it to appear that I needed it."

"I was there with you through a lot of those times."

"I know you were and, somehow, I thought taking your husband would give me some sort of vindication for the way I was treated."

Shayla stood up, walked over to the window, and opened the curtains. At that moment, she knew without a doubt that it was not a good idea to have accepted Rhonda as a client. "What did you want vindication for, Rhonda?"

"I was treated like a throwaway by my mother, a hand-me-down by men, and a stepsister by you."

"That is a flat out lie. I never treated you like a stepsister. I treated you like the sister I never had. You were my best friend. I went to bat for you when your mother threw you out. I fought with you on the playground. I told you my every secret. I asked my mother to take you in and give you things that could have easily been given to me. I loved you."

"You did help me. It's just that...."

Shayla cut her off. "Help is a stranger giving you directions or someone opening a door for you when you're carrying groceries. I didn't help you. I opened my heart and shared my life with you. So, let me ask you something about your vindication, Rhonda. Did having a child by my husband give you all the vindication you needed? I hope so. I hope that now you can live your life with all of the joy and vindication that you felt you deserved."

Rhonda looked down at the floor when she answered, "No. I didn't."

"I'm sorry to hear that. I hoped after all things were said and done that at least you would be happy now."

"Shayla..."

"You hurt me to the core. Do you hear me? To the core."

"I know and I've suffered for my mistakes!" Rhonda said between sniffles.

"Found out Titus wasn't all that he was caked up to be, huh?"

"I could sing the same blues you used to sing to me about him not being at home, how he talks to me, or how he treats me. What good would that do right now?"

Shayla was completely out of her bounds of being a mental health physician, so she collected herself and attempted to return the appointment to any semblance of professional.

"It will not do any good now. I apologize for talking to you that way. You came here today for counseling and that's what you deserve as a client. From this point forward, I will treat you like any other client."

That statement seemed to bother Rhonda, but she agreed. "Okay."

"Tell me why you are here today."

"I left home a week ago trying to figure out what in the hell I'm doing with my life. I mean, what's left of it. I thought if I visited the people I hurt, people that truly loved me, I could at least get some closure." Rhonda shot her a desperate look. "But, if you see me as just one of your clients, I will go now."

"If it makes you feel better, I do not hold any grudges against you. I have moved on with my life and I'm in a good place, a very good place. I have already forgiven you for what you have done, so I hope that gives you closure," Shayla said and turned to look her eye to eye.

A tear slipped from the corner of Rhonda's eye and she quickly wiped it away. "I am sorry for everything."

"Well, there you have it. No hard feelings."

"No," she said nervously. "There is one more thing I need to tell you and I don't know how to say this."

Rhonda stared off into space as if she was pondering how she was going to deliver the devastating blow.

"Take your time and say what is on your mind."

"I'm dying of cancer."

"Cancer?" Shayla heard what Rhonda said. However, her brain did not register to accept it as truth. "What do you mean you are dying?" she asked with a frown.

Rhonda crossed her arms and began rubbing her shoulders as if they were cold. "I mean what I said. Doctors say I have only months, if not weeks, to live. With treatments, I could live longer, but I don't want to risk living my last days feeble and weak. I just want to go in peace."

Shayla stood frozen in place. She was barely able to get the next question out. "What are you saying to me?"

"I'm saying I'm sorry for the bad things I've done to you and I'm asking for your help in my final days."

"You mentioned doctors and treatments. What stage is your cancer?"

"It's stage four. The doctors are not sure what the primary is because it has spread to several places."

"Oh...No!" Shayla said. "I...I'm so sorry." She could not believe what she heard. Memories of their friendship flashed before her eyes. All of the good times and bad times were as vivid as yesterday as she stood there looking at the shell of a person that was once her closest friend. "Are you sure there is no treatment that you can take?"

"There is no treatment that I want to take. I have come to terms with my fate."

"Does Titus know?"

"No, and he doesn't care about anyone but..." Rhonda fought back a tear as brief glimpse of remorse rushed over her. "That is my business, so don't tell him anything! These meetings are confidential right?"

"Yes, they are," Shayla assured her, knowing it would be hard for her to keep that promise. "You shouldn't keep this from your husband. There are other people's lives at stake. For Christ's sake, you have a baby to think about."

"That is why I'm telling you, Shayla. You are the only person I trust with this information. The only person I feel will look out for my best interest."

"I'm flattered you think of me that way," Shayla said incredulously. "But, after all that we have been through, I'm not sure I'm the best person to put that type of faith in. I'm just being honest."

Rhonda stood up and walked over to the window to stand beside her. She looked out at the scenery for a second, and then turned on her heels. With pain in her eyes, she said, "If I could place my feelings directly in your heart, I would, but I can't. As the pages of my life have turned and with all that transpired, I simply say I miss you."

A knot formed in Shayla's throat as she looked away. Quiet as it was kept, she missed her, too.

Rhonda continued, "The things that happened made us both who we are today. I stand here with my laundry list of problems and you stand here in the middle of a prestigious office with the wonderful life that you made for yourself. The life you deserve, by the way. If I'd been a better friend, we'd be traveling the world, visiting our favorite places, and living the dreams we used to write about in our journals, chapter for chapter."

"We could have done things like that, Rhonda, but you had other plans."

"Please let me finish," Rhonda pleaded. "My life has been a rollercoaster of misfortunes and I know your life has its downsides, too."

Shayla said, "Yeah, but I made the best out of it. That's what women do."

"You have and you are doing great for yourself." Rhonda smiled. "I wronged you, but fearing that each breath you take may be your last makes a person think about what is important."

Shayla touched her shoulder. "There is no need to relive the past. Let's talk about help that you can get now."

"The past is exactly where I need to revisit. I have to right my wrongs before my time is up." Rhonda started coughing and Shayla rushed get some Kleenex, and then back to her side.

"You have apologized. The rest is for God to sort out," Shayla said when Rhonda's coughing stopped.

"My dearest friend, I have peeked over my shoulder and adored you. I have cried because I needed you. I have been lifted up and dropped because I wronged you and so many others. I am a work in progress and God is molding me daily. My awareness may disappear again, but at this moment I am aware of my wrongs and ready to right them."

For the first time since Rhonda arrived in her office, Shayla really looked at her. Not a glance over for outward appearance, she really looked at her all the way down to her soul and what she saw was her old friend. Rhonda said, "I read a passage you wrote to me when we were in high school. I felt it deeply and strongly. I remembered those nights of adrenalines highs and passionate thoughts that would captivate our minds and take us around the world for miles and miles, even though we had not left your home on Bibb Street. Then, I took one look at my child and remembered she was born out of lust for your husband. It dawned on me that I lost my mother, I lost my best friend – a person who treated me like a sister, and, worst of all, I lost myself. In talking to God, he revealed to me that everything I've done has been no mistake. It has molded me. Though I am ashamed of the things I have done, I would do it all over again simply because I don't wish to change *His* will. He wrote the story that I'm living and thus I must suffer and rejoice no matter what."

Shayla was in awe at the words coming out of Rhonda's mouth. Helping her would be an obstacle, but she was happy for her spiritual progress. She walked around to her desk chair and sat down.

"It sounds like you have done some soul searching," she said, tilting her head to the side, trying to read Rhonda further.

"I have my reasons," Rhonda said as she walked back over to sit in her seat. She picked her purse up and sat it in her lap. "So, are you going to help me?"

Rhonda asked once she was sitting down and eye to eye with Shayla.

"I will. You have several issues you are dealing with, so I need to know exactly what it is you want me to help with the most."

"My mother treated me like shit. I don't want to be remembered as the same kind of mother to my children, or even worse die and leave them alone in this world with a man who does not value women, like Titus. Help me figure out what is best for my family before I...well, in case anything happens to me soon."

Shayla looked at the desperate look on Rhonda's face and knew without a shadow of a doubt that she would help her. "Okay, I will help, but on one condition."

"You name it."

"You will have to do the things that I ask of you. No exceptions. I can only help you by getting to the root of your problem and you may not like digging to the roots, but that is where the solutions lie. While I cannot help you with your medical treatments, other than advise that you do what your oncology doctor advises, I can help you deal with the psychological, psychiatric, and psychosocial issues you will face during your illness."

Rhonda took a deep breath and began to wring her hands together. "You call all of the shots, but that's not all, Shayla."

Even though she was sure there was nothing else Rhonda could add to the equation, she prayed against and prepared for another bombshell at the same time. "What is it?"

"I just found out I'm pregnant, again."

"You're what?"

"I'm pregnant and there is a possibility that Titus isn't the father."

Shayla was floored at her admission. True to form, Rhonda Jackson, now Rhonda Wilson, was on the scene with a jug full of gasoline. The woman was known to have bombshells dropping everywhere she went and that day was no different.

"How do you know that Titus is not the father?"

"He has not been home long enough to get me pregnant and when he is there he is not intimate with me." Before Shayla could get her next question out, she continued, "And, if you are wondering how I could be this sick and get pregnant, I didn't do it on purpose. I didn't find out I was this sick until a month ago. I went in for vomiting and found out that I was pregnant. I thought it was the pregnancy causing me to lose weight, until I found out I had terminal cancer. Even though I'm in my second trimester, I have not been able to eat much and what I do eat I throw up."

The pregnancy made Shayla rethink her position. Rhonda had so much drama and she did not know if she could deal with it all. Rhonda's problems could affect her emotional stability. "Would you be open to seeing another doctor?" she asked. "I really think that would be better for you."

"No. If you don't see me, I will not see anyone."

"There are plenty of good doctors I can refer you to."

Rhonda stood up and gathered her purse. "I don't trust anyone but you. If I walk out of these doors without your help today, I will not return."

"Rhonda, you need to be reasonable about this."

"Please, sis. I need you."

A feeling that reached all the way down to the pit of her stomach told her that she should not touch Rhonda's case with a ten-foot pole. "I don't know. I'll have to think about it," Shayla said with reluctance.

"Well, while you are thinking about it, here is my number in case you need to get in touch with me." Rhonda placed her card on the desk. She put her purse on her shoulder and walked out.

As Rhonda walked out of the office, Shayla said, "Hey...come back next Wednesday. Same time." She had to help her. It was her duty.

Chapter 12

Rhonda

After leaving Shayla's office, Rhonda sat in her rental car almost fifteen minutes before she picked up the phone. The call she was about to make to her nemesis, she hoped, would mend a 10-year rival.

She found Gladys LaQuinn's name in her contacts and pressed the dial button. Gladys' upbeat voice with Hispanic undertones cheerfully answered on the third ring.

"Holla?"

"Uh, hi, Gladys. This is Rhonda."

"Rhonda who?" she said, quickly reverting to her all-American, beat-a-sistah-down voice.

"Rhonda Wilson."

"As in the Rhonda Wilson who married Shayla's husband?"

"Yeah," Rhonda said, trying her best to keep her attitude checked. "I'm glad you answered. I was hoping that your number hadn't changed."

"After hearing your voice on the other end of my phone, I'm going to look into getting it changed soon. Why are you calling me, Rhonda?"

"You and me...we haven't had a good relationship since college, but we tried to be cordial to one another anyway for Shayla's sake. I want to apologize for the way that I disrespected our friendship and for the way I put you down while you were dealing with James. You were going through a lot and I was anything but a friend to you."

Gladys laughed as if David Chapelle was in her living room doing a private comedy session for her. "You are too funny! I mean, here we are in our thirties and now you decide to be sorry for shit you did in high school and college. Well, at least you got around to feeling bad for what you did."

"Yes, I am sorry Gladys!"

"That is good. You should be sorry. Instead of kicking me, you were supposed to lift me up when I was down. I'm up now. Thanks for nothing."

"That is the reason why I'm calling you. It is hard for me to apologize to people, but I am asking for your forgiveness because I know I was wrong."

There was a long and uncomfortable silence, so Rhonda said, "I just don't want the day to come that you read about me in the newspaper and I hadn't had a chance to tell you that I appreciate you as a friend and I love you."

Thrown completely off guard, Gladys asked, "What is wrong with you Rhonda? It has to be something major for you to call me like this."

"Don't worry about what is wrong. Just know that I want to do what is right."

"Well, thanks for doing what is right, for once," Gladys said.

"I'm not going to hold you. Kiss your babies for me and tell Maverick I said hello." Rhonda ended the call before Gladys could respond.

Chapter 13

Shayla

"So," Shayla said as she entered Lissa's office at lunchtime. "The all mighty Seth has struck again. What has he done to you now, girl?"

"Huh?" Lissa looked at her as if she was totally clueless.

"You've been on lockdown all week. What kind of spell has he put on you?"

"What do you mean?" Lissa snapped her notebook close and gave Shayla a side eye.

"Pretend to be clueless if you want, but you haven't called me one time to go to lunch the past week."

Lissa laughed and put her notebook down on the desk. She started tapping on the keyboard. "I've just been busy."

"Oh, well, I understand being busy. That's why I put all of my work aside and came by to see what was going on with you."

"I've been right here working on this new software project. So busy, in fact, that I have hardly seen the light of day." It was true that she was working on different projects. However, her number one project was Mission Become Seth Baker's Fiance. She dared to tell Shayla about that mission, so she continued tapping away on the keyboard as she spoke. "Yeah, it's been keeping me so busy that I haven't had time to talk to anyone. Just a working away."

"I heard that," Shayla said playing along. "I've been pretty busy, too. Residency can be overwhelming."

Lissa didn't look up from her keyboard. "I can believe that."

Shayla sat down and crossed her legs in full investigative mode. "What's up with the guy you met in Baltimore?"

"Nothing much. Just...taking it easy."

"Taking it easy, huh?"

Lissa tapped even harder on her keyboard. "Yeah, just doing me, you know."

Shayla picked up the notebook sitting on the desk and started turning the pages. "If that is the case, why have you written 'I Love Seth' all over this notebook?"

"Dang, you are like an overbearing big sister. Stop being so nosey, Shayla!"

"I'm not nosey, just observant. But, for real though, just because of a fling during a business trip, you should *not* be daydreaming about how much you love him."

"Give me that," Lissa said and took the notebook away from Shayla.

"Think about it, he does this conference every year and every year there is a number of women looking for a nice time with a handsome and powerful man."

"I already thought about that."

"So, you know that you could just be the booty of the year for 2013."

Lissa was visibly agitated by Shayla's intrusive advice. "I was not born yesterday. I understand how the dating and sex game goes. Thank you very much.

"Alright. I will back out of your business. I just don't want to see you get your hopes up too high just to be let down. You are making me wonder if you really are about that life."

Lissa didn't know whether to laugh or kick Shayla out of her office. "You watch too much YouTube."

"Maybe I do, but I am led by my spirit in everything that I do or say. I was joking, but this is real. I see the look you have in your eyes when you talk about him, so I know where you are emotionally. I had the same look when I was unsure if my first husband loved me. I was unsure if he wanted to be with me. I was unsure of everything. I know you have only known this guy for a short time, so time will tell everything you need to know. I just don't want to see you get hurt. All I am saying is that where love and lust is concerned, we all can use a nudge back to reality sometimes. My advice is to proceed with caution. Take it slow. He ain't going anywhere, unless he is supposed to."

"Thanks and I hear you, but I'm following my heart on this. If I'm wrong, I'm wrong. No harm, no foul."

"At the end of the day, I'm still going to be your bestie, lunch buddy."

"Yep," Lissa said logging out of her computer. "He says he's coming to Atlanta this weekend, so I'll see him then. Maybe I can talk him into staying for a while."

"Go on girl. You've got that man using his frequent flyer miles already!" Shayla gave her a high five.

"He has a house in Atlanta, so he was planning to come here anyway."

"Sounds like you picked a winner, at least where his finances are concerned."

"I know, right?" Lissa said and laughed, waving her pen as she spoke. "I plan to be all up and through there this weekend, swinging from the chandeliers."

Shayla shook her head and laughed. "Just nasty! Come on, let's go to lunch."

Lissa put her pen in the holder on her desk. "Where do you want to go?"

"How about the new Japanese grill in downtown?"

"Give me a minute to write a note for my secretary and I'll be ready."

"Okay. Meet me at the car," Shayla said as she exited the office.

As soon as she walked out of the building, she bumped into a man wearing a long, brown coat and shades. She would not have thought much, if anything, about the accident had he not looked at her as if he was about to speak. Instead of speaking, he quickly looked away when their eyes connected. She could not put her finger on it, but something about the way the man looked at her just was not right. She searched down the street in the direction he went but, just as quickly as he appeared, he vanished.

An unshakable, eerie feeling came over her as she walked to her car. In fact, it was the same feeling she had when the old man put her bag in the console on the airplane. In a rush of nervousness, she hurried to her car, jumped in, and locked the doors. Once she gathered her composure, she drove to the front door to wait for Lissa.

Chapter 14

Lissa

Even though she told Shayla she had to leave a note for her secretary, her mind was hundreds of miles away from her current situation. She could only think about the passionate look in Seth's eyes when she last saw him. During that vulnerable moment of intimacy, she broke down and professed her love to him.

"I love you," she told him that night. She had every reason to believe the sacred three words that rolled so easily from her lips were also in his heart. He hadn't actually said the words, and it was probably too soon for them to be on her mind. Yet, she was sure 'I...love...you' was just around the corner for him as well. While waiting on him to return her spoken sentiments of love, the thick silence in the room nearly sliced her heart like a knife.

He simply smiled at her and said, "Say it again."

99

His request to hear the words again were enough to send her to climax.

"I love you," she said, once again, with ease. It was her truth. She could not reconcile those three words with logic, but they definitely fell from her lips.

"I have strong feelings for you, Lissa," was his reply once their bodies disconnected. He threw in a lifeline in the middle of her sea of emotions that she caught and held onto for dear life. "I care about you a lot," he added.

Taking in the moment, she engaged the sultry and mesmerizing look in his eyes, which told the story that his voice would not. He felt the same way. He loved her.

His admission of *care* was interpreted as more than the caring expression strangers gave to one another as passersby on a busy avenue. That care was somewhere up there next to love. Somewhere up there next to commitment. Somewhere next to the utmost respect.

With her mind at ease, she snapped out of her daydream reaffirmed in her feelings for Seth.

"Shoot! Shayla is waiting for me in the car," she said and shook her head. She stood up to gather her purse and cell phone. "I can't think straight when it comes to that man."

Just as she was about to put her glasses on her face, an empty vase sitting on the windowsill caught her eye. The weekend was approaching, which meant she would get to spend more quality time with her boo. She couldn't wait.

Who says there is a time limit on when a person begins to feel love? she questioned and wrote a quick reminder to have something special delivered to his job.

She walked out of the office and to the front of the building. As she got closer to the car, she noticed Shayla looking around as if she were paranoid. "Hey girl, you look like someone just mugged you or something."

"No, just sitting here waiting on you. What did you have to do write a dissertation report before you came down? I've been waiting on you for almost twenty minutes," Shayla said once Lissa put her seatbelt on.

"Calm down. I had to finish writing the ideas down for the client I was working on when you came in, so I wouldn't forget. But, you look shaken up. Are you okay?"

"Just saw some weird looking guy that spooked me, but I'm cool. I think I'm going to change our lunch spot to our favorite place. I'm in need of comfort food."

"Gladys Knight Chicken and Waffles?" Lissa asked rubbing her belly. "Sounds awesome, but I might have to stop hanging with you for lunch. I have a figure that I'm trying to hold together. The extra pounds will not look good on me when I'm swinging from the chandeliers this weekend."

"Whatever," Shayla laughed. "It's grub time."

They rode in silence to the restaurant. Lissa scrolled through her phone as Shayla fought through Atlanta lunch traffic. Minutes later, they were seated and looking over the menu.

Shayla spotted what she wanted to eat, sat her menu on the table and said, "When I say that drama is knocking on my door, I mean drama is knocking at my door."

"You don't do drama. It must be time for me to dance at somebody's wedding."

"I'm afraid that once again there is serious drama brewing in my world. The surprise bombshells that landed in my lap today scare me and hurt at the same time."

Lissa placed her menu down on the table. "I hope I'm ready for this. What is going on?"

"Do you remember when I first started shadowing at the psychiatry center?"

"Yes, the first day I asked you to go to lunch you were an emotional wreck. You had so much on your mind, you released a lifetime worth of baggage during that one hour. I was so glad when the toxic people from your past were out of your system, because I was running out of jokes to keep you smiling during our lunch dates."

Shayla smiled at Lissa. "You are the best." She paused, and then continued, "Speaking of best, the friend that betrayed me has moved to Atlanta. She and Titus have moved here."

"You mean, the friend that stole your husband?"

"Yeah...her." Hearing Rhonda described that way rubbed Shayla the wrong way.

"Oh, I see."

"She came to my office Wednesday for an appointment and looked horrible. She's lost about fifty pounds and she says she has cancer."

"Oh, God! That is terrible."

"On top of it all, she is pregnant again and does not know who the father of her baby is."

"Shayla, you need to shut the front door immediately! That is a hot and steamy ass mess."

Confiding these confidential details in Lissa was in defiance of the HIPPA confidential law. However, given their history, she knew it was also unethical to take Rhonda on as a client. In this situation, Lissa was the counselor to the counselor.

"I'm not sure that I can help her," Shayla said as worry lines stretched across her forehead. "I am not sure I should help her."

"I can imagine it's hard to help someone who stabbed you in the back, and then laughed at your pain. I think the question I would ask myself is why she chose to come to you for help?"

"She has stage four cancer and wants to right her wrongs in case she dies."

"Do you believe her?"

"Yeah, I guess so. The last thing I want is for my family to have to go through some bull, because I'm trying to fix Rhonda's life."

The waiter who'd taken their orders ten minutes earlier brought their food and asked, "Is there anything else I can get for you?"

"No this looks great," Lissa said, and then looked at Shayla for agreement.

Instead of agreeing, Shayla's eyes were affixed across the room and as big as two silver dollars. She looked as if she had seen a ghost. "My God," she said.

Lissa looked around trying to spot what had Shayla's attention. "What is it?"

"Speak of the devil and she will appear. The lady sitting over there in the corner is Mrs. Jackson."

"And who is Mrs. Jackson?"

"Rhonda's mother." Shayla put her glass down. "I'm going to go over there to talk to her."

Lissa grabbed her arm. "What are you going to say to her?"

"She needs to know what her daughter is going through and more importantly, she needs to know *she* is the reason."

Chapter 15

Tom

I know her favorite restaurant. I know what booth she will choose to sit. I know what she is going to order. I know how she is going to hold her drink. I know the conversation she is going to have with the waiter. I know at what point her bladder is going to be too full that she will have to go to the restroom. I know the exact amount of time that she will let the sink run as she is washing her hands. I know that she prefers paper towels over the dryer in the bathroom. I know that she will return and only eat a few more bites before paying the check. I know this woman inside and out, Tom thought as he sat on the opposite side of Gladys Knight Chicken and Waffles. The order of chicken wings and waffles in front of him were cold as ice. He was a lot of things. Hungry for food was not one of them. However, his taste buds whet at the site of her.

"You're the best girl in the world. There will be a time when you are my therapist and I will be your only client," he said as he took a sip of his black coffee. The hot, dark liquid slid down his throat warming him to the core.

"I think today is the day to let her know how I feel," he said underneath his breath. He scooted back in his chair and stood up.

"No, I'd better hang low," he said realizing that it was still too soon. His patience was getting thinner and thinner. Tom sat down, put his hand up to his head, and took a deep breath. "What would I even say to her?"

He stood up again and walked briskly in Shayla's direction, thinking that what to say would come to him when it was time.

Chapter 16

Shayla

Mrs. Jackson sat in her booth looking as gorgeous as ever. Her makeup was flawless. Her skin hadn't aged one day in the past ten years. Her clothes were immaculate. Her attitude was regal.

As Shayla approached the table, she knew convincing this perfect-looking creature of any wrongdoings would be a task. She would be lucky if she got her to listen to anything concerning Rhonda.

Reaching the table, Shayla hugged her neck in excitement. "Hello, Mrs. Jackson!"

"Hello dear." The older woman looked her over thoroughly. "Do I know you?"

"It's me, Shayla," she said stepping back.

"Excuse me, mama," a man said rushing by after she apparently bumped into him.

"No, excuse me, sir." When she turned around to apologize, she only saw the back of the man's head as he rushed out of the restaurant. Shayla shrugged her shoulders and turned her attention back to Mrs. Jackson.

Mrs. Jackson took her glasses from around her neck and put them on her eyes. "Why it *is* you, Shayla. How has life been treating you, honey?"

"It's been pretty kind to me. How about you?"

"I've been pretty well. What have you been up?"

"Well, I went back to med school and I'm doing my residency now. Plus, I'm married again."

"That's wonderful! I know your mother is proud. You have grown into a beautiful woman, as well. Time has been treating you kind."

"Thank you, Mrs. Jackson. You don't look a day over thirty five," Shayla said with a smile.

"Flattery will get you everywhere." Mrs. Jackson said as she put her glasses back around her neck."

"What are you doing in Atlanta?"

"Shopping and good soul food, of course," Mrs. Jackson said returning a hearty smile.

Shayla pointed to the empty seat across from Mrs. Jackson gesturing to take a seat. "May I?"

"Sure."

She decided to start with small talk. "Are you still living in Opelika?"

"I bought a new home after Travis died, so I am not in the same place, but I am still in the area." Sadness covered her when she mentioned the name of her late husband.

Shayla placed a hand atop of hers. "I'm sorry to hear that. I didn't know Mr. Travis passed away."

"Yeah, he's been gone a year. God bless his soul. But, I'm blessed and besides the problems I have with my hip whenever it rains, I'm in good health." Mrs. Jackson's smile became vulnerable when she asked the next question. "Have you seen Rhonda lately? How is my baby doing?"

Shayla wished that she could say, 'Everything is just whoopty-do and swell,' but she couldn't. Rhonda needed a miracle to happen and she needed it soon.

"Before today, Rhonda and I have not been on speaking terms for at least five years."

Mrs. Jackson gasped in surprise. She tilted her head to the side and asked, "What do you mean? You girls are sisters."

"Yeah. That was what I thought, until things transpired that sent our friendship into a downward spiral."

"These things must be terrible for you not to speak for five years."

Shayla nodded. "Yeah, it was pretty bad."

"You are two peas on a pod. Everything she does is because you did it first, and vice versa. When she was a young girl, she would not eat breakfast if you were not eating. She loves you like a sister. Whatever it is, I know you girls can patch it up."

Shayla remembered those days more vividly than Mrs. Jackson. It was when Rhonda became an adult that she expressed her love for her in a way that felt like hate.

"I felt the same way about her. I guess all things change with time," Shayla admitted.

"What happened?"

"Where should I start?"

"Start at the beginning."

Shayla began to tell Mrs. Jackson how she confided in Rhonda problems she was having in her first marriage. Then finally, she told her the main reason that they were no longer friends. "She had an affair with Titus and to make matters worse they are now married and have a child together."

"A ch-child?"

"Yes, you are a grandmother and your son in law is my ex-husband."

If looks could tell a story, Shayla would say the last 25 years of Mrs. Jackson's life traveled past her eyes as if they were on a movie screen. Mrs. Jackson went through a range of emotions from guilt, sadness, indifference to joy. "You mean to tell me that the only child I have in the world has a child and had I not came to Atlanta today to shop and end up sitting in this particular booth at this particular restaurant at this particular hour, I would not be any the wiser?"

"Mrs. Jackson, you and Rhonda don't have the most proper mother-daughter relationship. That is the reason I wanted to talk to you. She needs your help right now, more than ever."

Mrs. Jackson dropped her head and shook it as Shayla gave her reasons that she should reunite with her daughter. The uncomfortable words poured from Shayla's mouth like a tragic poem.

"I have to see her," Mrs. Jackson said with tears flowing down her face. "I have to see her now!"

Chapter 17

Shayla

"Baby, I'm home," Shayla said as she entered her front door. It was after seven in the evening. Her body was tired. Her mind was moving one hundred miles a minute.

"It's our Queen," Antonio said to his son.

"Our Queenie!" her son said as soon as he heard her voice. Tyler ran to greet her with Antonio close behind.

Her husband hugged her tight and kissed her lips, while her son held onto her leg. Tyler reached his tiny arms up wanting to be picked up. "My kiss, too," Tyler said in a soft, angelic voice. "Pick up and get my kiss, too."

"Hold on little guy. You will get your chance. Big guys get their kisses first, and then the little guys," Antonio said as he patted his son on the head.

Shayla looked at Antonio and playfully rolled her eyes. She then kneeled to pick up Tyler. "Aw! You know my little guy comes first, too, don't you?" she asked as she began to rub noses with him. He immediately burst into laughter when his mother's nose touched his.

Tyler looked at his father with a smile and said, "Me come first, too."

"Yes, you do son." Antonio patted his son on the head again and led them both into the kitchen where dinner was waiting on the table.

Shayla followed her husband into the kitchen. "Honey, you have been in here throwing down," she said.

"I sure have," he boasted, flicking his collar. "I told you as long as you are doing your residency I will handle everything in the house. I want you to focus on the finish line and I am going to do my part."

On the table was a bowl of grilled corn, asparagus, sautéed chicken, a pitcher of iced tea, and a bottle of red wine. Shayla looked down at her stomach, which was still stuffed from lunch.

"I had a big lunch, so I'm not sure how much I can eat and still fit into my pants tomorrow, but I cannot pass up your sautéed chicken and asparagus." She giggled as she rubbed her stomach.

Tyler jumped down and sat at the table. "I hungry, mommy."

"Okay, buddy, let's eat." She looked at Antonio, and said, "But, I'm eating light."

Dinnertime was an important time to her family, so she nibbled on the food her husband prepared. For the next thirty minutes, they talked about each other's day and events they had planned in the near future. Rhonda's impromptu visit to the office eventually became the highlight of their conversation.

"Did she say how long she had to live?" Antonio asked.

Her eyes went to the floor. "Months, if not weeks judging on how she looks."

"If that is the case, how are you going to handle it?" he asked.

How am I going to handle losing Rhonda? She sat in thought for a minute. She had been perfectly fine being distant from her for the past five years. Yet, somehow the thought of her dying changed the game.

"I will have to think about how I am going to..." she said, pausing because of the horrified look on Antonio's face. "Why are you looking like that, babe?"

"Who the hell is that?" he asked as he stood up and walked toward the window. About the same time, there was a loud thud against the kitchen window.

"What are you talking about?"

"I think someone was looking in our window." He opened the window and looked out seeing the shadow of a large statured person running across the backyard. The person dashed behind a row of bushes when Antonio rushed to the side door and flew out of the house.

Shayla went to the door and looked out with little Tyler close on her heels. He cried and asked, "Mommy what wrong!"

She picked him up and held him tightly in her arms. "Don't cry honey. Daddy will take care of it."

Antonio ran toward the area the shadow disappeared, the person stood up, and started running down the street. The chase was on. Antonio chased the mysterious person for nearly a block. Meanwhile, Shayla called 911.

"Oh, God! What is happening?" she said as she waited for the operator to pick up the phone. A few minutes later, she finished giving the dispatcher the rundown of the situation and hung up the phone.

Antonio walked back into the house visibly shaken. Through labored breaths, he said, "I better not catch that motherfucker snooping around here again."

"Did you see who it was?"

"No, I didn't get a good look at him, but they were dressed in all black and whoever it was is a track star. He must have run a four flat around the block."

"Well, the 911 dispatcher says a police car is on the way," she told him. Her heart was racing.

"Good." He was angry, frustrated, and wished that he could have gotten his hands on the peeping Tom. "He was looking through the window, watching us eat dinner. I kept thinking that I saw something, but when I would look back at the window it would be gone. Then, I saw the whites of someone's eyes piercing through the window. That's when there was a loud thud against the window."

Shayla looked around in fear of her own surroundings. She took Tyler to the other side of the room to play with a pile of toys lying on the living room floor. She walked back to Antonio and asked, "Who would do something like that at our house?"

Antonio raised his shoulders. "He was at least five feet ten to six feet. Maybe brown to light skin. It was too dark to make anything else out, but when I get my hands on him, it is going to be trouble. No one comes snooping around my family."

"Just when I thought this day could not get any crazier," Shayla said, pacing the floor.

"Ever since I heard of Titus and Rhonda moving to Atlanta, I knew things would get out of hand."

"Are you suggesting that they had something to do with this?"

"All I am saying is that they better not have anything to do with this. When it comes to my family, they are playing with fire. I will protect my family, by any means necessary," he said. The look in his eyes, she'd never seen it before and hoped not to see it again.

"It could be a kid pulling a prank," she said, hoping her gut feelings were wrong.

"It could be," Antonio agreed. "Let's just make the police report and try to finish dinner," he said.

Within seconds, police lights flashed in front of their house. They filed a police report, locked the house down, and went back to the dinner table.

Chapter 18

Seth Baker

"I hate to leave, but I have to go. I have a midnight flight," Seth said and placed a kiss on her cheek.

"Do you have to go? Can't you just stay for one more night?" she asked and planted her signature tongue-laden kisses, one by one, on his lips.

He thought long and hard about whether he actually had to leave at that time, or if he could stay for a while.

It was extremely hard each time he had to leave. It would be his dream to stay holed up in her apartment for one more day. When he left, he'd dream about her until he came back, and just like that their time was up.

With a long sigh, he strongly considered her proposition. "I wish I could stay here with you forever.

However, I'm not sure my business would survive if I followed my wishes."

"I know you have work to do and so do I. I guess I will let you go...for now," she said as she buttoned his shirt.

Then, he watched her button her own housecoat. She pouted as she walked behind him into the foyer. She got his jacket out of the closet and helped him into it. When he walked out of the front door, he turned around and saw a tear in her eyes.

"Goodbye for now," he said before turning to walk away. He did not like to see her that way. It touched him deep.

"For now," she agreed as he walked down the steps. Her door closed behind him. Their encounter officially ended.

I need to break this off. Seth thought things were too hot and too heavy with her. There was something about Lissa McDaniels that kept him coming back over the past three months. He shook his head in attempt to shake her out of his system.

The first thing that he did when he got into his car was dial Jennifer. He avoided her calls for the past twenty four hours, so he knew the call was not going to be pleasant.

"How is my favorite lady doing this morning?" he said when she answered the phone.

She paused before answering. The pause was her familiar way of addressing him.

"Lis...Jennie," he almost misspoke. "Please say something."

"After I have been trying to reach you for the past day, now you want your favorite lady to speak at will? Are you okay?" she asked.

"Good...as long as you are." He made a statement, as well as question at the same time.

"Oh, I'm so good over here that I don't know if it could get any better. Are you sure you are okay, though?"

As a general rule, it was best not to give up information that could be used against you. Seth used that rule accordingly. Instead, he asked as many questions as possible and tried not to sound suspicious. He wanted to find out what she knew. "Why do you have such an attitude? Why are you asking me am I okay?"

Jennifer said, "I'm a business major who graduated the top of my class, cum laude. I close million dollar deals with the same ease that I close my closet after I get dressed in the morning. I am the most sought after business consultant in Atlanta when it comes to putting businesses on the right track. I am the cream of the crop. People seek me out and bid top dollar so that I will work with them and not their competitor."

"You are that and more, honey," he agreed. "What gives me the honor of hearing your accolades and credentials this morning?"

"Like so many others who are not on my team, you insult my intelligence. I know when a deal is going sour before the first drop of sour hits it. One hundred percent of the time, I protect my investments before the end is near."

Seth's palms were sweating, but he could not show weakness as Jennifer would sense it before he could count to three. "Stop talking in riddles, and say what is on your mind."

"I just want you to know that the biggest riddle in our marriage is solved. Now, you go on and have a safe trip back to Baltimore." With that said, she hung up the phone, leaving Seth with the busted look on his face.

When he tried to call her back, she did not answer, so he slowly pulled out of Lissa's apartment complex parking lot with more than a night of good loving on his mind.

Chapter 19

Lissa

It's Business, Never Personal

Jennifer walked into Lissa's office early the next Monday morning. Her face was glowing and she had a huge smile on her face when she said, "Good morning, Ms. Lissa McDaniels."

Lissa smiled back. She was happy to meet with Jennifer so that they could begin work on the last leg of their project. She also welcomed the distraction from thinking about Seth. Lately, her work ethic was slipping and a meeting with Jennifer was sure to get her back on track.

"Good morning, Jennifer!" Before getting started, she acknowledged how beautiful her colleague looked. "You are glowing this morning. Did you have a hot date last night?" she teased.

"Not exactly a hot date." Jennifer did not look at her when she answered. She placed her briefcase on the floor beside her seat, opened it, and removed some documents. She reviewed each document before placing them on the desk.

"Whatever happened needs to happen more often. You look great today."

Jennifer's face was serious as she looked eye to eye with Lissa. "Thanks for the compliment, but I'm sure it would happen more often if my husband were free long enough to make it happen," she snapped.

Lissa did not understand where Jennifer was coming from, so she was thrown off by her remarks. "I'm not sure I understand what you are saying."

"If it is okay with you, may we get down to the business at hand?"

"Fine with me," Lissa said with a nod of her head.

"How did the presentation to the implementation team go last week? Were they satisfied with the changes that I suggested?" Jennifer asked.

"As a matter of fact, they liked the changes and felt they could be put in effect with little to no problem. There are a few glitches that have to be worked out on our end. Other than that, we are on track to move forward."

"Great! Let's get go over the ideas that I've come up with for postproduction and even a few marketing ideas. I'd like to go over these things thoroughly and without interruption, since I plan to leave at noon today," Jennifer said.

"Sure thing." Lissa gave her a knowing look. She thought the business savvy woman was going to get more of whatever had her glowing that morning. She hoped to be glowing the same way in the next few days when Seth returned to town.

The ladies discussed many ideas and wrote many notes. Before they knew anything, the eleven o'clock hour was upon them.

"Jennifer, I think we covered enough ground today. Follow up from this meeting will keep me busy until next Friday," Lissa said with a huge laugh.

"We have gone over a lot," Jennifer agreed.

"So, how about we schedule our next meeting for Friday morning and go from there?"

"That sounds excellent!" Jennifer packed her briefcase, and then looked at the stack of papers on Lissa's desk. "When I get going, ideas flow left and right. That should be enough to keep you so busy that you don't have time for much of anything else."

Lissa looked down at her note pad and agreed. "I can see that. As long as they are fruitful for Naytek, I will take all the ideas that you come up with."

"That's the spirit. Next Friday at nine a.m. is good for me, so I will see you then?"

Lissa checked the date on her calendar and marked it as occupied. "It's a meeting," she said. "See you next week."

When Jennifer gathered her belongings and left out the office door, Lissa took a deep breath and tried to brush off the nagging thought of Seth's brief visits and him not allowing her to go to his Atlanta home.

He promised he would take her, but when the time came, he backed out again. She seriously needed a lunch date with Shayla. "Hey Shayla," she said after dialing her number.

"Hey, you sound like you need a lunch date," Shayla said.

"You know me too well." Lissa stood up and looked out of her window. The busy street below matched the many thoughts racing through her head.

"I need to get out of loony land for a few minutes, too," Shayla said as she closed her laptop and started stacking the papers on her desk.

"You need to stop. You know you love your job."

"I do love it. I just need to get away for some sisterhood therapy."

"I will be there in fifteen minutes."

"I'll be ready."

***

"What reason did he give you for not taking you to his house?" Shayla asked as she cut her organic chicken salad sandwich in half.

"He didn't exactly give me a reason. He just kept saying let's stay at your place. Then, when I told him I really wanted to go, he acted like he didn't feel like driving over there. Even when I offered to drive, he turned me down saying that a real man drives his lady around."

"Did he hit you with the 'your place is as good as mines' line?"

126

"Yeah...and the next thing I know I am pinned against the wall in my bedroom not caring if I was at his place or mine."

"So, you really don't have a problem with him not taking you to his place?" Shayla asked before taking a bite of her sandwich.

"I want to go and see his home, especially since he said he would take me. It is more about the principle than me seeing the house. I have invited him into my world and showed him everything that I have to offer. I want an invitation into his.

"If that is what you want, why did you reward him breaking his promise with hot, butt-naked sex while being pinned against the wall in your bedroom?"

Lissa pursed her lips together and folded her arms. "That's a good question?"

"It is a damn good question. For you to be happy, you require more than he gave you. Yet, you engaged in one of the most intimate things two people could do. You rewarded him, even though he did not meet the requirement."

"I don't know! It's like I lose all of my good sense when I am with him."

Shayla shook her head. "I'm going to need you not to do that," Shayla said with a laugh. "I want you to start asking yourself questions before you give up the precious goods. Before you give in to your vaginal needs and wake up the next morning angry because you allowed yourself to accept less than what you require. If you stop and ask yourself questions, at least, you will have thought it through. You have to learn to make decisions that you are good with the next day."

"That's deep, Shayla," Lissa said with an eyebrow raised. She took a sip of her coffee and thought about what she said.

"It's not really that deep. If you require that he be a man of his word, you should not lay down with him when he tells you half truths. It's not his fault how he treats you after that. It is yours."

"I see what you are saying. But, maybe I'm being too persistent about seeing his house. Everyone does not move at the same pace and he may not be ready for all of what I'm laying down. I am willing to wait."

"There is nothing wrong with waiting, as long as there is balance. Make sure you are not the only one waiting for what you want."

Lissa took a deep breath. "I'm rationalizing now, huh? Thanks so much for always keeping it real with me, Shayla. You are a great friend."

"That's what friends are for."

"Look at us. We are supposed to be here giving you a breather from work and here you are dealing with my issues."

"Oh honey, don't worry about it. I'm supposed to pull your coattail and let you know when your slip is hanging. It is your place to pull up your slip or continue to let it hang. I trust that you will take the advice I gave you, and pull your slip up."

Lissa knew Shayla was giving her a subliminal message, so she knew there was more to her last statement than met the eye. "Are you saying I am wrong for waiting on him to invite me into his space?"

"Look, I'm going to tell you this as plain as I can say it. You've opened your home, body, and, for all intents and purposes, your heart to him. Meanwhile, he is on leisure time to extend the same to you. He is probably right to take things slow. You should follow suit. When relationships – new or old – are unbalanced, you can wait for it to be an unwanted outcome, a messy one. Also, when you start out accepting little things in the beginning, imagine what you will be accepting in the middle, and let's not talk about the end."

Lissa sat quiet for a minute as sadness stretched across her face. She knew Shayla was right. She also knew the feelings she had for Seth Baker were too strong to be set aside with a girlfriend pep talk.

After a few minutes of awkward silence, Shayla changed the subject. "So, let me tell you the new drama I have going on in my life. Last night, some creep was peeping through our kitchen window and Antonio had a high speed chase down the street, following the person."

"Did he catch him?" Lissa asked, half interested and half stuck on their previous conversation.

"No, but we filed a police report. It was so creepy that I am almost to the point where I'm afraid to be in my own home."

"Do you think Rhonda showing up has anything to do with it?"

"Rhonda? I hadn't even thought about Rhonda being a suspect." Shayla had successfully kept a positive disposition about her up until that moment.

For the next thirty minutes, the ladies sat and chatted about the goings on in their life. It turned out that they both needed an ear to bend.

Chapter 20

Rhonda

"While you are dealing with this, continue to be close to your spiritual connections. Pray to God for healing. Turn all of your problems over to *Him* and let God sort them out. You haven't forgotten about how mighty our God is, have you?" Shayla said at her second session with Rhonda.

"Yeah, he sure is mighty." Rhonda said in sarcastic amusement. Seconds after putting her purse on her shoulder, it dropped to the floor beside her chair. "He's *mighty* alright."

"He truly is!" Shayla said, closing her eyes as she was carried away by the greatness of her Heavenly Father. "He brought us a mighty long way and gave us a chance at repairing our broken friendship."

Rhonda sat in her therapy chair, looking at Shayla. The distress in her face was heavy.

"I'm dying and you want me to sit here and glorify God? Spare me from having to hear of *His* mighty goodness today. And, excuse me if God is starting to feel mighty heartless, mighty unfair, and mighty depressing."

"Don't speak that way, Rhonda. Just the other day, you were talking about what God meant to your life. You were filled with hope that only *He* is able to bring. When I went to lunch that day, I saw your mother and she even..."

Rhonda looked at Shayla as if she had grown tentacles. "My mother?"

"Yeah. Mrs. Jackson really wants to see you and meet her granddaughter."

"Of all people to bring up in the middle of talking about God's mightiness, you bring up my mother?" She fought the tears that began to flow down her eyes.

"Rhonda, I..." Shayla said before being cut off.

"She has never cared about what happened to me, so there is no need for her to start today."

"You have to get things right with her, while you still have time."

"All I have to do is stay black and die, and I'll be dying soon enough," Rhonda said with an attitude. She picked up her purse once again and stood up abruptly. She took three steps toward the door, and then turned to face Shayla. "Why would God allow me to lose everything that mattered to me and add things to me that would hurt me? I have a death sentence and I'm scared and hurt."

"Rhonda, there is a difference between God's lessons and his blessings," Shayla said from her seat. "This could be *His* way of getting you to soul search and have the relationship that you always wanted to have with your mother."

"Well, I will be at my hotel searching for my soul. I will definitely need to find it before I consider sitting down to talk to my mother."

"You really don't get it do you?" Shayla stood up and walked over to the door to stand beside Rhonda.

"I don't get a lot of things. That's why I'm here."

"You have issues that go deeper than the things that you have done to hurt people that love you. It's because you loved your mother and she hurt you. Hurt people hurt people."

"You just leave my mother out of this or things are going to get even uglier than they are now. You have no clue of how ugly."

Shayla softened her tone. "You only have to talk to her when and if you are ready. However, I implore you to do it for your daughter and your unborn child. They will need her if anything happens to you."

"I will think about it." Rhonda walked out of Shayla's office without looking back.

Chapter 21

Lissa

Three Months Later

It was about seven in the morning and Lissa was up doing her morning stretches. It was her and Seth's three-month anniversary and she planned to get a shower and start breakfast before he came over to visit. He called and told her that he would be there at 8 a.m., so she prepared anxiously for him to arrive.

However, all of her unwavering loyalty, deep passion, and willingness to put her livelihood on hold for another moment staring into his sexy brown eyes was shattered when her phone rang. Picking up the cold portable phone from the receiver, she pressed talk.

"Please, tell me you are standing on the other side of my door right now," she said playfully as she walked into her bedroom to pick out her clothes for the day.

No one said anything, so she said, "Hello?"

An unfamiliar, deranged sounding woman yelled, "Bitch! Don't call my husband, text him, or do so much as think about him, you home wrecking whore! I better not..."

Lissa stopped dead in her tracks. Her mouth flew open in a stuck-on-stupid position. Her head immediately began pounding, as if she was suffering a horrid brain freeze from a cold drink. She was not dealing with any woman's husband, so she did not understand why the woman was calling her.

"Excuse me," she managed to squeak out in a voice that was not her own.

"You heard me bitch!" the woman yelled.

Pacing the floor, Lissa found the strength to say, "You must have the wrong number."

Silently, she prayed the woman's husband was not the man she'd been making the sweetest love to for months. Seth had done a number of things to make her suspicious, but she didn't want to believe it. Namely, he still had not taken her to his house in Atlanta.

"Oh, I've got the right number, and you hear me loud and clear. Leave my husband alone!" she said again, so loud and commanding that Lissa began to tremble.

"I'm...I'm not the one..." She defended herself. "I am not the one you are looking for."

She believed the woman had the wrong number, until a roaring, familiar voice in the background made her stop and listen.

The fact that some lunatic acting woman was on her phone at seven o'clock on a Saturday morning did not hurt one bit. What broke her world into two pieces was hearing Seth in the background pleading with this woman not to leave him.

"She doesn't mean anything to me, Jennifer. Please, please, hang up the phone and let's talk about this," he said.

Lissa was in a state of shock and awe as she listened to his pleas.

"I am telling you there is no other woman in the world that means as much to me as you do."

His begging made her stomach turn He sounded the most pathetic she'd ever heard him. It was as if he suffered with cottonmouth and the woman held the key to all of the world's water reserve.

"I love you," he said, as he continued to plead his case to the woman.

There they are, Lissa thought. Those three words she so patiently waited to hear him say. Those three words that sealed the deal in relationships. Those three words that so easily fell from her lips when they made love. Those three words that so easily rolled off his tongue...to his *wife*. He loved the woman and he had no problem shouting the expression from the top of his lungs. It didn't even matter that those three words would crush Lissa. She couldn't count on her fingers how many tears threatened to run down her cheeks because he had not uttered those same words to her.

"Listen, whatever this *thing* is you two have going on, it's over! Stay away from him, Lissa." The woman paused and spoke in a lowly threatening tone to add extra effect to her next words, "You have been warned."

At that point, Lissa caught the voice of the person on the other end. "Jennifer?" she said before she could catch herself.

"In the flesh and if you know what is good for you, you will forget this whole situation with my husband ever happened."

"Are you threatening me?"

Jennifer's voice dripped with contempt. "No sweetie, I am promising you that you will not like the outcome."

The next words were from Seth. It was obvious that Jennifer had shoved the phone to his mouth and dared him not to echo her sentiments. He said, "I don't want to see you anymore, Lissa. It is over!"

"Tell her everything," I heard Jennifer say.

"I don't want you. Jennifer is the only woman for me. I want my marriage. What we had was some kind of…fling," he said. "I have to be faithful to my wife."

The sting of his words was felt all the way down to her soles. Though he sounded like a wounded animal, his words were loud and clear. He did not want her anymore.

Lissa almost felt sorry for him when he let out a little sniffle. *Her man* was crying and in some twisted way she felt bad for him. However, hearing him plead to a woman he held in higher regards forced stinging hot tears to run down her cheeks. Then, a violent shaking of her shoulders erupted.

One week prior, Seth slid in between her sheets and made sweet love to her like there was no tomorrow, and definitely like he didn't have a wife. He made her feel as though the only two people that existed on earth were her and him. She believed those feelings. They were her truth.

As Lissa pondered the contrast between the two events. The last night he was in her bed. The early morning call from his wife. She was haunted by memories of candlelit conversations, throaty moans until the midnight hour, bouncing from soft sheets on the bed to the bathroom counter, and ginger strokes that sent them both into lovemaking ecstasy. Monday morning flowers and intriguing late night phone conversations gave her strength.

Slow and calculated, Lissa said, "Seth, how could you dismiss me like a two-bit whore after all that we have shared? Am I really nothing to you?"

"Lissa...I..." he paused. She could hear his wife fussing and cursing like a sailor in the background. There was no doubt that Jennifer was the commander in chief of their household.

She could tell by the way he responded he would rather be anywhere in the world than stuck between the woman that he vowed to love forever and ever, Amen, and the woman he had been engaging in a fiery love affair with for months. For the moment, the fact that he was silent was enough.

"I just can't do this anymore. It's wrong and my wife needs me," he said. His words finally finding their way to the tip of his tongue. I was sure Jennifer was close on his heels providing the bulk of the strength he needed to finish that statement. "I'm sorry, but you...and...I should have never happened," he added, barely above a whisper as if he was actually afraid to hear the terminal things coming out of his mouth.

Before Lissa could respond, the phone line went dead and she was left alone. Left to drown in the deep end of life's pool without a life preserver. It would have been different if he prepared her for this day. He had not given her any swimming lessons for those types of waters. She assumed that he was single. In the short time she was involved with Seth, she never so much as thought that he could be married.

"How could you do this to me?" she asked the phone that lay in the palm of her hand, lifeless. Sharing fears, dreams, and hopes with another person was not supposed to end like this. She stared at the phone needing him to call back and tell her that the last ten minutes of her life was a prank call. .

The next morning, when he knocked on her door with tears in his eyes, a bouquet of the most beautiful roses, and a box of chocolates as a peace offering, she wanted to slap the shit out of him. She wanted to read him like a book and ask him what kind of cheap woman he thought she was. She wanted to deny his entry back into her world. Instead of doing any of those things, she stepped aside and let him in.

Chapter 22

Shayla

Shayla convinced Rhonda that a meeting with Mrs. Jackson would help resolve the resentment she harbored and allow her to move forward. Even though Rhonda warned the meeting would be anything but pleasant, she was hopeful that she could bring the two women back to a good place. Before Rhonda arrived, she was sitting in her office talking to Mrs. Jackson.

"I'm just so thrilled that this is finally happening. I've been hopeful since I saw you at the restaurant and now I'm getting another chance to see my only child! Do you know what this means to me?" Mrs. Jackson asked.

"When she gets here, we will start by catching up on what you two have been doing since you last saw each other, and then I will take it from there."

"Sounds marvelous to me." Mrs. Jackson smiled with the joy a mother has the first day she brings her child home from the hospital.

"I know it means a lot to you. But, I would not put too much stock into today's session. I had to do a lot to convince her to meet with you and she barely agreed. This is her first time seeing you in a long time, so don't expect too much. Think of it as a start."

"I trust that all will be fine," Mrs. Jackson said leaning over to touch Shayla's desk. "I prayed that all will be fine and it will."

"Oh, but all is not fine, mother," Rhonda said, interrupting her mother as she entered the room. "It stopped being all fine the day you chose Mr. Travis over me."

"Rhonda, come in and have a seat," Shayla intervened.

When she saw the surprised look on her mother's face, Rhonda let out a laugh that was calculated and evil. "Remember me? The girl that you threw away."

"Oh, Rhonda," Mrs. Jackson said before letting out a loud cry. Her eyes were weary as she looked at her daughter's emaciated body. "Come on in here and sit down, so we can talk."

"Since you both want me to have a seat, I'll stand," Rhonda said in defiance.

"Please baby, have a seat," Mrs. Jackson pleaded.

"I said, I'll stand. Now, let's get on with this little meeting. What do you want from me?"

"Well, Shayla said we could catch up on what we have been doing since we last saw each other, and then she would guide us from there," Mrs. Jackson said as she accepted a tissue from Shayla.

Rhonda looked at Shayla. "Is that what she said?"

"Yes, please, have a seat. I plan to mediate this meeting like any other family session," Shayla said.

"For the third time, I'll stand thank you," Rhonda said to Shayla, and then rolled her eyes back to her mother. "How convenient it must be for you to prance up in here and let Shayla try to clean up your mess, again."

"What do you mean by that, Ronnie?"

"Don't you Ronnie me! It's Rhonda to you."

"Well, Rhonda. Tell me what you mean by that statement."

"You sit here and hide behind Shayla's shield, thinking she will make everything all right. When I was a teenager, she made everything all right by taking me in when I had nowhere else to go. I mean, you should have seen her fixing things for you, mom. She ran home and begged her mother to let me move in when you kicked me out in the streets. She kept in contact with you to tell you how I was doing for years when you didn't have the decency to check on me yourself. Why did she have to do all of that?" Rhonda put her pointing finger on her lips and looked pensively. "Oh! Because your perverted husband wanted to touch me at night and I wouldn't let him."

Mrs. Jackson stood up. "That is nonsense and you know it's a bald face lie!"

"Now, there she is." Rhonda looked at Shayla. "That's my real mama, Shayla. We all know what gets a rouse out of her. Her man." Turning her attention back to her mother she said, "Well, mama, I thought it would. The truth hurts like a motherfucker and if you would be real with yourself for once you'd know that the reason he always said that I was causing trouble was because I fought him when he tried to come into my room when you were not home. The trouble was that when he went to sleep one evening I put a knife to his neck and threatened to cut out his jugular if he ever touched me again. That was the reason he told you I had to go. That was the trouble you kicked me out to the streets like a rabid dog for."

"Ronnie, I am so sorry for whatever happened that would make you think Travis would treat you that way."

"I never met a sorry bitch that wasn't sorry, so that's one thing we can agree on."

"I have to intervene here," Shayla stood up and walked around to stand beside Rhonda. "First of all, will you please have a seat, so that we can all be on the same level?"

"And you, you are sitting in here with MD-Resident on the wall, while I am sick, depressed, and destitute. We are *not* on the same level." Rhonda fixed her eyes on her mother. "And that's probably because your mother actually gave a fuck about you when you were younger. Not like my fancy mother, sitting here in her expensive hat and purse. She always knew how to make things look good on the outside."

Shayla put her arm on Rhonda's shoulder. "Stop using that kind of language or I am going to have to end this meeting."

Rhonda said, "I wouldn't dare want to be the cause of ending such a touching reunion." The scowl on her face was deafening, but she sat down.

"Rhonda, please, listen to me. I..." Mrs. Jackson begged for her daughter's attention as tears flowed down her cheeks.

Rhonda said to Shayla, "What's the point in talking to a woman who has lived her life as if she didn't know me, much less birth me? We've come this far without inconveniencing each other, why should we start now?"

"Because it is never too late for second chances. Because forgiveness is powerful. Because carrying around all of these bitter feelings is not healthy for you or your children."

Rhonda folded her arms and let out a deep sigh. "I am not bitter, I'm pissed. There is a difference."

Shayla said, "Without bringing up specific incidents from the past, I want you to turn to your mother and tell her what you are upset about today. When you woke up this morning, what about your life was the most upsetting?"

"There are a lot of things I'm upset about. Do you want me to just pick one?" Rhonda asked.

"If you had to choose the thing that bothers you the most, what would it be?"

Rhonda looked at her mother. "The fact that my daughter would not recognize her grandmother in a lineup." Mrs. Jackson dropped her head in shame. Her tears at this point were constant. "As long as you are married to him, she will never know who you are. I will not allow her to experience her grandmother choosing a pervert over her."

Shayla asked, "Mrs. Jackson, how does that make you feel?"

In an attempt to save face, Mrs. Jackson took a deep breath and held her head high. "I didn't know."

"How could you know? You didn't take the time to talk to me to find out what I was going through. You just assumed I was a problem child, without trying to figure out the root of the problem. You abandoned me months before you put me out," Rhonda said.

Shayla asked, "Knowing how Rhonda feels and hearing her experiences, Mrs. Jackson, what would you like to say to Rhonda?"

"It hurts. I feel like a failure as a mother, and as a person. I feel like I wish I could redo it all, but I know I can't. Right now, I just want another chance to do right by her." Turning to face Rhonda, she said, "I promise this time will be different."

"That all sounds fine and dandy, but there is one thing that you cannot redo and that is my memories. My memories of laughter, the first time I saw Santa Claus and my first bike ride were stripped away. It's like I blocked any happy times from my mind. All I remember is being ripped from my mother's home and told never to come back," Rhonda spoke calmly.

Mrs. Jackson reached over and touched Rhonda's hand. "Please, let me be there for you now."

"Everyone can make a change for the better, Rhonda. Your mother is offering an olive branch," Shayla said, attempting to convince Rhonda of her mother's renewed commitment to a relationship with her.

"Mr. Travis is gone," her mother added, hoping that would convince her. "He died a year ago."

Rhonda searched her mother's face. The sadness in her mother's spirit when she spoke of his death made her nostrils flare. She removed her hand from her mother's touch and laughed, mimicking Sophia from the *Color Purple*. "Well, Hallelujah! I knowed there was a God." Then, she looked at her mother and sarcastically said, "Aw, excuse me. What am I thinking? Sorry for your loss."

Her mother held her head high and looked away. "I am not a perfect woman. I have made my fair share of mistakes." She looked back at Rhonda. "But, I am here fighting for the only person I have left in this world. If it means being humiliated, so be it. I owe you that."

Rhonda looked at her mother and for the first time she had a look of compassion. Instead of allowing memories of bad times consume her, she allowed better memories to enter her mind. She saw the woman who held her hand and walked her to school on her first day. She saw the woman who told her how beautiful she was before church on Sunday morning. She saw the woman that she loved before she hated.

Since Mr. Travis wasn't a physical wedge between them, Shayla prayed there was a chance that a truce could be established.

Chapter 23

Shayla

Good Morning Honey

"Are you making any progress with her?" Antonio asked, wrapping his arms around his wife's waist.

"She is making good progress. She is even gaining a little weight. Her doctors say that she is holding up very well, considering her condition. She started the divorce process and overall seems to be doing better."

"Glad things are going okay," he said as he walked to the adjoining mirror and began to brush his hair.

"Counseling Rhonda is not as bad as I thought it would be," Shayla said, curling the last portion of her hair. It was Friday morning and she was attempting to get ready for work in between cuddles and kisses from Antonio.

"That's good. If anyone can help her, it's you. She's in the hands of the best. As long as the situation is healthy for you, I support you." He turned her around to face him.

"Surprisingly, I am okay. It's been months and she still refuses to see Titus. She says the only way she will talk with him is if he has questions about the divorce papers."

"She is a cold piece of work, huh?" Antonio said as he started to shave his face.

"Not as much as she used to be. She did let her mother keep her daughter while she is working on her health and finalizing the divorce."

"That's probably best. And the fact that Titus has not come around is best for us. I don't want him coming around causing problems."

Shayla hugged him from behind and he turned around to face her. "I'm not worried about him," she said.

"Well, I can't help but to keep him under my radar. I intend to protect my family, by any means necessary."

She touched his face. "Look at my macho man. Always looking out for us. I love you."

"I love you, too. I will always look out for mine, and you are mine." He kissed her lips and began to rock side to side with her in his arms.

"I look out for you, too." She hugged him tight.

"So, how about we both call in late and really look out for each other?"

Shayla's arms fell from his neck. She slowly walked out of the bathroom and began straightening up the bedroom. "I would love that, but my first appointment is at nine."

On her heels as she walked away, he cornered her as she began to leave the room. "Too bad. I was thinking you might have some time for a little of this." He pulled her into a kiss. "And, a whole lot of this." He placed kisses all over her neck.

"Lord, why do you feel so good?" she asked once she found the strength to push him away.

"Come on, Shayla."

"I can't." She honestly had to leave in the next few minutes to make it to work on time. "I have to go to work. Mrs. Jackson is my first client today. She is an early bird, so she's probably there waiting for me now."

He walked to the mirror, readjusted his tie and ran his hand over his beard. "I guess you get off easy this morning. Tonight, will be a different story."

"I hope so," she flirted, picked up her briefcase and headed toward the kitchen.

"Have a great day changing hearts and minds," Antonio teased when he came into the kitchen with his keys in his hand.

"Funny, but you have a great day, too, babe. You have changed my heart and mind forever. If you were not a part of my life, I would not be the woman that I am today."

Once again, he pulled her close. "What kind of woman are you today?"

"The kind who loves herself some Antonio Davis so much that I can just taste him."

"You realize that your nine o'clock appointment will be sitting there waiting on you if you keep boosting my ego."

"Go to work, man!" she said pushing him toward the door. "As soon as my last appointment is done, I'll be in the car headed home. That should be around noon."

"Great, I'll meet you here. That will give us hours before Tyler has to be picked up from daycare."

She looked at the passion burning in her husband's eyes. It was only on days like that she wished she did not have a list of patients waiting for her. "It's a date," she said before kissing him and watching him walk to the door. "I'm going to fix a smoothie, and then I am right behind you."

"Okay, see you in a few hours," he said before closing the door.

She put in ingredients for her smoothie and turned on the machine, smiling as she pressed the start button.

Chapter 24

Tom

He watched her morning routine. He loved everything about it. The way she put on her bra. The seemingly cautious and regal way she slid her panties up her legs. The wondrous way she applied lipstick to her copious lips. He wished he could be the tube, gliding back and forth across her lips.

Watching her prepare for work was the highlight of his day. What he saw that morning, however, was far from routine and pissed him off to the highest of pistivity.

Typically, Antonio was an early bird. He pulled out of the driveway by 7 a.m. every morning. It was baffling to Tom that he was still home well after eight o'clock. He'd stayed home late attempting to seduce the woman that Tom loved.

"It's one thing he gets to wake up next to the woman of my dreams. At least he could get his ass up and go to work when he is supposed to." Rage built in Tom's voice as he spoke.

The shift in routine was his sign. It was time Shayla knew how he felt. "I'm going to go in there and show her why she belongs to me. I am going to show her the magic that we share. Today is our day," Tom said as he peeked through the privacy fence to see Antonio pulling out of the driveway. "I will declare my love for her today!"

When Antonio turned the corner and exited the neighborhood, Tom stood at the side of the house for a long while, mulling over whether or not he had the nerve to face her.

You can do this man. He heard a loud and unsympathetic inner voice tell him. *Just go for it for once in your life. You can do it.*

He put one foot in front of the other and walked toward the front door. The voices in his head were right. It was time he declared his love for Shayla.

Chapter 25

Shayla

Shayla poured her smoothie into her favorite tumbler and grabbed her briefcase. Rushing out the front door, she was startled when she bumped into Ms. Morris before her foot hit the porch. Shayla's voice cracked as she asked, "Ms. Morris, what are you doing here?"

She quickly glanced around to see who drove Ms. Morris to her house. There was no trace of a vehicle or driver, which added to her puzzlement.

"I had to talk to you," Ms. Morris said. Her voice was distressed.

"Did you come in a cab?" Shayla asked, eager to know how her patient ended up on her doorstep.

"No. I didn't come in a cab. My neighbor dropped me off at the corner. Please, don't be upset with me for coming. I just had to talk to you today."

Shayla softened up a bit. "I'm not upset, just surprised that you are here. How did you find out where I live?"

"I looked you up in the phonebook. I wouldn't have come if I didn't need your help. Let me in and listen to me, Mrs. Davis!"

"Is everything okay?" Shayla asked stepping aside to let the woman into her home. The fact the woman was at her home in the first place was startling. But, she trusted whatever she needed must have been urgent.

Ms. Morris did not answer her question. She simply shook her head from side to side and walked into the house.

"What is bothering you, Ms. Morris?"

"I need to find out who is taking my social security check," the elderly woman said. Her voice ripe with anger. "You're the only one I can trust to help me get this straight. Will you get it straight like you did when I was in the hospital?"

Shayla loved her clients. God knew she did. However, that surprise visit rubbed her about three wrong ways. She didn't like the fact that she showed up unannounced at her home. She was even more disappointed that the woman's request was not urgent.

"This is not something we should be handling at my house." She looked at the confused woman and added, "Ms. Morris, do you understand that you are *not* to come to my house for things like this?"

"I know," the woman's voice was flat. "I knew you would be upset about me doing this, but you are the only person in the world who treats me like a human being. Everyone else is out to get me. Even my neighbor who brought me here is stealing water from my house. He thinks I don't know that his water meter is hooked to mine."

"Have you called the Social Security office?"

"I called them, but the girl on the phone is a dummy who thinks I am the one who is crazy. Told me that my check was at the bank, but when I called the bank they said I haven't had a deposit this month."

Shayla looked at her watch. "I will check into it later today. I have to be in the office in less than fifteen minutes, so my secretary will handle it when I get there."

She didn't want to leave Ms. Morris hanging, but her options were slim. Either she could stay at home with her, find her a ride home, or take her with her to the office.

"Have a seat," Shayla said choosing to stay with her until she could get her help. The woman's clothes were mismatched, her hair was matted, and she was sweating like she just ran a marathon.

The two women sat on the sofa and Shayla took out her cell phone. "I'm going to call someone to come get you."

"I don't want to go back home! I don't have running water, because my neighbor has stolen it all. And, some nice little guy came by today and turned off my power. They said I ain't been paying the bills. How am I gonna pay the bills if people are always stealing my check? I need you to find out..."

157

She put up a finger and said, "Hold on Ms. Morris. Just a second," as she dialed her office.

"It's a great day to find your happiness. How may I help you," her secretary said when she answered the phone.

"Shelly, it's Shayla." She looked at Ms. Morris standing in the middle of her living room. "An emergency has come up this morning, so I am going to miss my first two appointments. Please, apologize to them for me and find out if they would like to reschedule. Matter of fact, just call all of my appointments for today and cancel."

Shelly's usual high-pitched voice was one octave higher when she asked, "All of them?"

"Yes, cancel all of them," Shayla confirmed. I'm kind of tied up with something else right now. "Also, will you call the disability office and see if you can find out where they are sending Ms. Morris' check? She is saying that she is not receiving it again."

"I will get on that right now."

Hanging up the phone Shayla took another deep breath. Her next call was to the hospital. "Hi, this is Dr. Davis, resident for the psychiatric service. I need non-emergent transport for Ms. Prichette Morris. Yes, she is a regular patient on the psych unit. She showed up at my house about fifteen minutes ago with a relapse. Yes at my house. Thank you." She gave them her address and some other details about the situation and hung up the phone.

"Would you like something to drink?" she asked Ms. Morris who was wandering around the living room

158

admiring pictures and home décor as if she were in a fine art gallery.

"No, thank you," Ms. Morris said seeming to have partially gathered her senses.

"Fine. I just called transportation for you. We are going to have to get you stabilized again with a short stay in the hospital. Meanwhile, we will find out what is going on with your money, so you can get your power back on and your finances straight."

The woman scanned the beautifully eccentric characteristics of the home. She walked around, looking at different items and touching each thing she found intriguing. "Thank you, sugah. I like your place. I always wondered what it would be like to be inside your house."

Suddenly, Ms. Morris was calm and collected. Something about her calmness was alarming. Shayla walked over to the window and looked out, hoping the transport team would hurry up and get there.

Ms. Morris stood beside her at the window and touched Shayla's hand. "I've missed you since the last time I saw you in the hospital."

Shayla moved her hand away and said, "You were supposed to call the office if you had any problems. Other than that, we are supposed to miss each other. That means you have received good treatment"

"I couldn't call. My phone is off. Everything is going up in smoke. I barely have a few dollars left in savings to buy food." Ms. Morris crossed her arms. "Why are you looking at me like I'm some sort of monster that you don't want in your house."

"I'm not."

"You're looking down on me, just like everyone else."

"Ms. Morris..."

"Don't Ms. Morris me, and I know all of your doctor talk, so don't even go there with me. That's the problem, you think I'm stupid. I've tried to show you how much I like you, but you brush me off and send me away. You think I don't know you're just like the rest of them. You don't care about me, or any of the other people like me. You just make money off us. You probably spent my social security check on this fancy house of yours." Her voice became louder with each sentence.

"We both know none of that is true. I do care about you and want you to get the best care," Shayla said in a soothing tone. "Now, you are going to have to calm down."

"You disappoint me, Dr. Davis." Ms. Morris, who had a humped over posture was gradually standing tall. She took slow, calculated steps toward Shayla.

Just as Shayla was thinking that she might have a struggle on hand with Ms. Morris, the doorbell rang. The transport team arrived as Ms. Morris was getting rowdy and she was able to talk the woman into going peacefully.

Chapter 26

Shayla

Relieved the morning madness had settled down, Shayla sank down into the comfort of her sofa. She contemplated going to work in order to get her mind off Ms. Morris, but she quickly slashed that thought. She was lying with her hand covering her eyes when the doorbell rang, again. She looked out the window and saw Antonio's car in the driveway and a sigh of relief flew from her throat. After the incident with Ms. Morris, she locked all three of the locks on her front door.

"Hey, honey!" she said in pure joy when she opened the door. A joy that was quickly replaced with surprise and disgust. "What are you doing here?" she asked the man who brushed past her and into the foyer.

He grabbed her hand and pulled her away from the door, locking and closing the door behind him. "From the look on your face, I can tell I'm the last man you were expecting to see today," he said in his want-to-be baritone voice.

The mad look in his eyes scared her to death. Her voice caught deep down in her throat. The only thing she could hear was the blood pumping hard through her temples. Her chest rose and fell hard. Her breaths were deep and labored.

As she stood there in shock that he was in her home, wearing all black and looking like he was about to rob the place, he looked around her house and nodded his head in approval. "This is a nice place you have here. It looks much better from the inside. I got to give it to you and ol' boy. You really have done well for yourselves. Everybody ain't able." He knocked an oil painting and a family portrait down from the table in the foyer. The items fell onto the floor and the glass shattered on impact. "Ooops. I'm so sorry."

She looked at the painting and then back to him. After the time she had with Ms. Morris, the last thing she wanted to deal with was another intrusion. Devoting her life's work to the mentally ill had upsides, but having to deal with days like that was a downside they didn't teach her about in school.

"James, why are you here?" she asked. He was her friend's ex-husband who not only was abusive, but was an All-American jerk. It had been five years since Shayla laid eyes on him, until she mistakenly opened the door.

For years, Gladys kept it a secret that she was abused. Up until she got an invitation to Florida for a weekend getaway, no one knew about the abuse. She ran into her college sweetheart during that trip and, from that day, she was reunited with the man she truly loved.

James was enraged when she left him. One night, he stormed into her office and attacked her. If it hadn't been for Maverick stopping by, he would have beaten her until she was unrecognizable. He was later sentenced to three years in prison for that attack. He took their divorce hard and even wrote Gladys a letter from prison promising to finish what he started.

"Why am I here?" he asked. "I'll tell you why I am here." He ran his hand across the table in the foyer and knocked off the remaining picture of her, Antonio, and Tyler.

"Stop it," she said, finding courage to fight back. "Do not put your hand on another thing in here!"

Ignoring her, he knocked over a figurine. "I'm here, because you messed up my life. You took away something that was important to me."

"James, no one is important to you but yourself. You abused someone that I care about. You messed up your own life."

He stepped closer to her and grabbed her by the arm, "It's funny you would say that I only care about myself. It's not true. I care about you. You know, three years behind bars gives a man a lot of time to think, and I wasn't thinking about her. No. She is free to live her life with that high society, college boy that she is with. I have my sights on an even better prize," he said, looking as if he could eat her with his eyes.

"Get out of my house, right now, or I will call the police! You have no right to barge into my house like this." She took one step toward the front door and was pushed hard into the wall.

"Don't make me show my ass on you. You have seen my work, so you know I will," James said grimacing. "I will leave when I'm good and ready. Now, I've been watching you ever since I got out of jail over a year ago and waiting for the moment I could let you know how I feel about you."

Shayla feared that her encounter with James would not end as well as the one with Ms. Morris. Watching him transform into a mad man in front of her face was terrifying. "James...please, leave," she pled.

"If you know what is good for you, you will go into the living room and sit down." She did not move, so he pulled out a blade and flicked it open. "Move!"

Like a prisoner on death row, Shayla walked into the living room taking every step like it was her last. She stood beside the sofa and a flashback of Antonio's car in the driveway made her heart beat faster.

"Antonio's car was outside," she said. "Was my husband out there?"

"Maybe, maybe not," he said with indifference as he rubbed the blade against his pant leg.

Fearing the worst, she asked, "Did...did you do something to him?"

"Nothing that you should worry your pretty little head about right now," James said, pushing through the nervousness that was attempting to stop his plan.

"James, I need you to tell me that you didn't do anything to Antonio."

"He'll be knocked out for a while, but he will be okay. Now, sit down and let's have some you and me time." When she refused to sit down, he said, "Sit yo' ass down before I make you sit down."

Shayla sat down on the edge of the couch and put her hands in her lap.

Once she was seated, he studied her for a long while. "You are so beautiful. I have waited for a long time for the opportunity to sit down next to you," James said.

"James, please, don't do this."

"Shut up!" he said and pushed her back on the sofa. He grabbed her face and kissed her long and rough, forcing his tongue through her closed lips and teeth. "Are you happy with your new husband, your new family?" he said once he broke the gruesome kiss. His body grinded hard against hers and the pressure of his body was firm. Not waiting for her answer, he placed kisses about her neck and face. "That bastard child of yours should have been mine. I want you to have my child."

She didn't want to weep and show a sign of weakness, so her voice was calmer than she felt. "Please, stop."

"Have you ever thought about me the way I think about you?" She didn't answer him, so he threw his head back and digressed, "I messed up. I should not have hit her the way that I did. I went too far, but a man should always rule over his household."

"You could have killed her," Shayla reminded him. "She ended up in ICU for three days."

"Yeah, but she had Maverick to help her soothe her pain. Who did I have? No one." He paused for a few seconds and then ran a finger up her arm. "Look, I don't want to talk about her. Today is about the awakening of us. When we came to live with you, all I could think about was you, night and day. Did you have feelings for me, because I felt it, too?" he asked.

She pushed him away and rolled from underneath him. When she attempted to stand up, he grabbed her arm.

"No, I do not feel anything for you! You're controlling, selfish, and violent. The way you treated my friend is the reason I could never like you as a person. I want you to leave my house, now."

He pulled her body close in an embrace. After seconds of inhaling the lovely scent he'd dreamed of smelling for over a year, he unbuttoned her shirt. "I know what will help you realize how much you want me."

"Get your hands off me!" she protested, attempting to pull away, but her arms were pinned down with the weight of his body.

A fierce struggle ensued as he ripped her shirt off and forced her bra down freeing her breasts. "Once we make love you will love me forever," he whispered as he took one of her breasts into his mouth. His brute strength held her into place.

"Please, do not do this."

"Just experience it, Shayla. It will be everything you could dream of. I promise. I have already dreamed of how beautiful it will be," he said as he intertwined his fingers with hers and held her hands down.

Hot tears ran down her face as she closed her eyes. Her stomach was tied in knots. She could feel vomit traveling to her esophagus. His grunts were louder with each passing second.

Grinding his pelvis against hers, he said, "I missed you so much."

"You are going to miss your brain matter if you don't get off my wife!" Antonio stood behind James with a 357 Magnum firmly pressed against his skull. "Get your bitch ass up!" he commanded.

James froze for a second before he jumped up and charged at Antonio. "You ain't shit, nigga," were his last words before the gun went off.

Everything moved so fast. As James lunged at Antonio, Shayla tried to protect her husband by pulling him back. At the same time, Antonio fired the gun. Shayla and James fell backwards landing on the couch.

"Shit!" Antonio said, pushing James away from her. "Shayla, baby, are you okay? Did you get shot?"

She opened her eyes and looked at him, but did not move. She then looked at James lying on the sofa with an obvious bullet hole in the center of his chest. Blood was flowing freely from the wound onto the couch. "I'm fine," she said. "I saw your car. I thought he'd hurt you."

"I was out for a while, but I'm fine."

"Before I let him in, I looked out of the window and saw your car. That's the only reason I opened the door. Then, he attacked me." She finally let the tears she held back flow. "I can't believe this happened," she repeated over and over.

"I'm just glad I came before he…" Antonio looked at James wiggling on the floor, gasping for air. "Before he did something worse to you. Look, I'm going to get my cell and call the police," Antonio said after hugging her tight.

"Okay," she said through tears. Before today, she had not given any thought about James, much less him doing something like that. Sitting there watching life leave his body as he lay on her sofa, her human instincts kicked in.

"James, don't you die!" she said applying pressure to his wound. "Help is on the way."

He looked at her and whispered the words, "I'm sorry, Shay. Tell Gladys, I'm sorry."

"Don't you die. An ambulance is on the way. Hang on."

"Tell…my…kids…I….love…." were his final words before his chest rose and fell for the last time.

As much as she hated him in that moment, she didn't want her godchildren's father to die on her sofa. She performed CPR on him for a few minutes before Antonio walked over and touched her shoulder.

"The police and an ambulance are on the way."

The look on Shayla's face told him that she could not save him. It was too late for the ambulance.

"He's dead," she said. When he pulled her close to him, she realized he was shaking like a leaf.

"It will all be over soon," he said attempting to console her.

"What was he thinking coming here like this?" Shayla asked Antonio.

"I don't know. He must have been hiding on the side of the house or something. I didn't see him when I drove up, but then out of nowhere he sneaked me when I was getting out of the car. He put a towel to my face and whatever was on it knocked me out. I heard him hollering from outside, but I couldn't move. It was like I was paralyzed. When I finally snapped out of it, I came in through the back and got my gun."

"He said he had been waiting for this day," she said.

"I bet he was the one looking through our window that night months ago."

"For Christ's sake," she said realizing that what he was saying was probably true. The thought that James had been creeping around their house for months spooked her even more than the thought of calling Gladys with the horrible news of his death.

Chapter 28

Shayla

"Here, put this shirt on before the police get here." Antonio handed Shayla a shirt as they stood in the living room, waiting for the police to arrive.

"Thanks." She took the shirt and looked down at the blood stains on her shirt. She dropped her head at the realization that a dead man was lying on their sofa.

Antonio helped her put on the clean shirt. "Babe, do not beat yourself up. It was self defense. There is no telling what he would have done to you had I not come in when I did."

She held him tight and cried while they waited for the police to arrive. "I don't understand why this is happening," she said through stinging tears. "Why is this happening?"

He held her in his arms. "Because some people are just evil, babe."

She yanked away from him in a panic. "Oh my God, Tyler! We have to get Tyler?"

"Sweetheart, he's still at daycare."

"Thank God you didn't bring him home. I am so glad he didn't witness this mess!"

"I will call Janessa and see if she can get him for us. It's almost four o'clock, so we have a little time before the daycare closes."

About the time Antonio pulled out his phone to dial Janessa's number, James' phone began to buzz. During the struggle, it had fallen out of his pocket onto the floor.

Antonio and Shayla stood in silence, staring at the glowing phone, which was loudly rapping *Warning* by the late rapper, Biggie. They watched the buzzing and glowing device as if it were a foreign object that had been propelled from a moving spaceship.

Shayla picked the phone up. To her surprise, Rhonda's face and number was displayed on the screen. "That's strange," she said. "Rhonda is texting him."

Seconds after the phone stopped rapping, a text message popped up. Then, there was another message and another. With great reluctance, Shayla pressed the message button and read the conversation.

I should have never listened to you. Your plan isn't working. It's been three months and we still haven't gotten any money out of them, the first message read.

Antonio moved Shayla's hand so he could see the screen, as another message popped up.

Do you think I want Antonio's baby growing inside of me. I'm barely eating a celery stick a day because of this stupid cancer lie and you're running around looking in windows? Yet, we still don't have any money. I'm tired of this shit.

At the end of the second message, Shayla's stomach was tied in knots. "What the hell is she talking about your baby growing inside of her, Antonio?"

"The hell if I know. I have not touched that girl, so she must be talking about another Antonio."

The phone buzzed again bringing their attention to the third message. Both of their eyes were glued to the screen.

How hard can it be to get Shayla to cheat on Antonio with you? My plan is already in motion to blackmail Antonio when I get the DNA test for his baby. Stay focused, and let's get this paper.

Shayla had no words. There she stood with James bleeding out on her white plush sofa and the love of her life being accused of impregnating the woman who stole her ex-husband.

When a new text came through, she didn't even read it. She handed the phone to him and walked off. "I just can't right now."

He turned up his face in a frown and said, "I do not know what they were up to, but I have not so much as seen Rhonda since we moved from Pine Mountains."

"Let's just not talk about it right now. There is too much going on to even deal with those text messages," Shayla said as there was a knock on the door.

"That's the police," Antonio said. He walked into the foyer and opened the door.

It was when the first policeman entered the house that Shayla remembered a dead man was laying on her living room sofa.

Chapter 29

Lissa

Love and Facebook

Finding out that Seth was married was a low blow to Lissa's ego. Staying on top of her game at work was becoming more and more difficult. It was even more difficult to have to sit across the table from Jennifer Sinclair-Baker with a professional attitude while the man she loved was Jennifer's husband. Jennifer handled it as business as usual, but Lissa was devastated by the whole ordeal. Whenever their meetings were over, she went to his Facebook profile just to look at his pictures. Even though the pictures did not provide her any solace, she tortured herself with them, anyway.

The photographs showed him chilling with friends, promoting his next workshop, and sharing motivational business statuses. What kicked her in the gut the most were pictures of him alone. They seemed to look directly into her soul. When she looked at those pictures, she did not see the man that conveniently forgot to tell her he was married. She saw the man that cared.

Scrolling through the albums, she found new pictures of him with his wife. They looked so happy and so in love as he caressed her in places he never publically caressed her. He looked lovingly into his wife's eyes in a way she only dreamed he would look at her. His simmering adoration for *her* turned her stomach. His wife was not a hidden treasure. She was a treasure he wanted the world to see.

I have to stop looking at this, she told herself.

The reminder that she was willing to change her life for him when he only considered her a weekend getaway package, threw her for a loop.

"I have no plans to leave my wife," he said the last time she talked to him. Then, the very next day he called her to vent about something Jennifer had done when she was hanging with her friends.

Just like the side chick, she was there to listen. She agreed with him and made him feel that he was right, even though he was wrong. She hoped the magic he shared with her would be enough to put a wedge in his marriage. However, it was apparent from the pictures that they were as strong as ever.

"I love you, Seth," she said. She meant it more than she ever meant anything in life. "I love you like my next breath." Continuing to see him after being confronted by his wife was a choice, loving him was not.

His response to her outpouring of love was anything but ripped from the pages of a romance novel.

"I don't know what you want me to say, I mean, I am a married man. I just can't be throwing those words around. I mean, I care. I care about you a lot," he'd said.

Her better judgment told her the long and empty response was not genuine, but she fought like a champion against intuition. She wanted the words to mean something, and to her they did. She believed with everything in her that his care and her love were on the same level. He cared about her. Cared. Who was she to argue with care?

As she sat and looked at the *love* he displayed for his wife, she realized how small of a morsel his care actually was. She went to her home page and saw a quote from Novelist Kerry Wagner that struck a chord. He wrote, *"When a man truly gives a shit, he'll hold your hand in public as oppose to only holding your ass in private."*

Maybe Seth's care was never meant to escape the four walls of a hotel room, or my bedroom, or any other place we had sex, she thought. She had so many emotions raging inside. She had so much she wanted to say, but no one to share those feelings with, so she wrote in her journal:

As I stare at my laptop searching for a gleam of hope that the man who once meant the world to me still has an iota of passion for me, I ask for forgiveness for being in love with another woman's husband. I hope to find enough strength to love myself more than I love him...

Signed,
Trying to Find Myself Again

Chapter 30

Lissa

Taking a trip to one of the finest restaurants in Georgia normally calmed her nerves. As soon as she walked inside the restaurant, a hostess ushered her to her usual seat. "Will you have your usual drink?" the waitress asked. Within minutes, her favorite drink was sitting in front of her.

"Now, that is what I call great customer service. Thanks!" Lissa said as the server walked away. She was half past ready to get her sip on. As she pressed her lips against the straw, her business cell rang, notifying her of a meeting in two hours. She was not looking forward to sitting through another meeting with the illustrious, Jennifer Sinclair-Baker, and she would have replaced her if her credentials did not precede her. After making note of the impending meeting, her personal cell phone rang, as well. It was Shayla.

"Hey, honey boo boo! How are you today?" she asked definitely feeling the effects of the early happy-hour drink.

"Lissa, I need to talk to you." Shayla's voice was grim and fully of anxiety.

Lissa's hand fell to her stomach. Her personal drama caused her stomach to be weak. She knew whatever Shayla needed to talk about was not good. She was sure of it. "Do you want to talk now, over the phone, or do you want to meet somewhere?" she asked, standing up and walking to a quiet corner in the restaurant.

"No, I would feel better if we met later tonight at your office."

"This must be serious."

"You have no idea."

"I'll be there at seven."

"Thanks."

Lissa ended the call and walked back to her table. A set of suits walked past her and she didn't even look up. Any other time they would have caught her attention and flirting would be inevitable. However, she had too much on her mind. She could not help but wonder what was bothering Shayla.

When she sat down, a caramel cream-colored brother who was with the group, caught her eye long enough to momentarily change her focus. He winked, and then quickly followed his group, as if the exchange never happened. Lissa took a deep breath and remembered the reason she was even at the restaurant – to give herself reprieve from the complications of her current relationship.

Over the next hour, she was served a tasty meal with various wine tastings and topped it off with her favorite dessert. Between sips of her drink, she strolled through messages on her cell phone. Pulling out her business planner, she jotted down notes.

As she was in deep thought checking messages, making follow-up notes, and devising plans to turn idle chatter into business, she felt a slight rub of her shoulder. It was Seth.

She gasped when she saw him. "What are you doing here?" she asked.

"I had a meeting with that group of guys," he pointed in the direction of the gentlemen she saw earlier.

"That figures," she said looking at the men who were all either smiling or waving at her.

"Yeah." He laughed. "So, what brings you here?"

"This is one of my favorite restaurants. I come here when I want to get away from the hustle and bustle of Atlanta. I like this place because it is quiet and calm. You know, unlike my life."

He did not address her remarks. "I find it ironic that you're here, and I'm here."

"Just a fluke coincidence It doesn't mean anything."

"It means we are together again. Another coincidence is that there is a hotel attached to this restaurant."

"We're here." She pointed to the sign inside the building. "But, we are not here *together*. Remember, you can't be seen in public with me."

"So, it's like that?"

"Just like that," she said with confidence.

He sat down in the free chair in front of her. "So, you think that you will just walk away from me like this and leave me alone."

"You are not alone. You have a wife who makes it clear to me every time I see her that you two are happier than ever, and expecting your first child. She'd better be happy that I'm as classy as I am. If I were trashy, I would forward all of the messages you send me on a daily basis directly to her."

"Messages that you don't have the common courtesy to answer."

"I will not answer to you anymore. You should find another unsuspecting conference attendee to fall in love with. Oh, excuse me, to fall in *care* with." She laughed at her own pain. She laughed even harder at the stupid look on his face. He really seemed surprised by her response and if she didn't know any better she would say he looked hurt.

"So, this is it?" he asked, touching her hand. "I don't want it to be."

"This is it. If you don't mind, I have work to do," she said, dismissing him like she did her workers at Naytek.

He stood up and fixed his jacket and tie. "Fine," he said and walked away.

Fine, she thought, as well.

On her last glance of him as he turned the corner, she knew he was a fine work of art, indeed. The only problem was that he was a fine piece of art that was off the market.

Chapter 31

Lissa

When Lissa made it to her office later that evening, Shayla had beat her there. She was pacing back and forth in the lobby, waiting for her when she arrived. She wore wrinkled jeans, an oversized sweater, and tennis shoes.

Lissa took out her keycard, so she could access the elevator. "What the what? Girl, you look like warmed over death."

"Not funny," Shayla said, with sadness in her voice. "And, please, no jokes today."

"Come on, let's go up to my office." Lissa swiped her keycard and they rode the elevator in silence. Once they arrived on Lissa's floor, she asked, "What is going on with you, Shayla?"

Shayla broke down crying. "James is dead. Antonio killed him."

Lissa put an arm around her and hugged her tightly. "Antonio killed someone? Oh, dear!"

"Yes, he did and it happened at our house."

"Who is James?"

"Gladys' ex-husband. He is dead," Shayla said as she walked away and began pacing, again. "You should have heard her scream when I called to tell her that the father of her children is dead."

Lissa asked, "Wait. Tell me what happened."

"Antonio killed him. He killed him right in front of me, Lissa."

She was not sure she wanted to hear anymore. At this point, she did not understand what her friend was telling her, but she didn't want to discuss something like that in the hallway. "Let's go in my office." She ushered Shayla into her office. When they were in the office with the door shut, Lissa said, "Antonio would not kill a fly, much less Gladys' ex-husband, so what is really going on?"

"It was in self defense. James came over to our house yesterday and attacked me. He actually was about to rape me before Antonio came in and shot him."

"I'm glad you are okay, girl. Why would James do something like that?"

"That is what I've been asking myself ever since it happened." Shayla cried until she started sniffling. "Antonio, Tyler, and I spent the night in a hotel. The thought of going back to the house spooks me. I don't think I'll ever be able to go back there."

Lissa handed her a tissue. "It is terrible what happened to James, but Antonio saved your life. He could have killed you."

"I know, but..."

Lissa patted a spot on the sofa. "Come here."

"This type of thing is not supposed to happen in my life. My husband is not supposed to kill the father of my best friend's children. This is not my life!"

"Unfortunately, it is. Some of the things we think will not happen in our lives are the very things that we have to deal with, so at this point, counselor, I would say it is time to deal with reality. James was a monster who tried to rape you and your husband defended his home with deadly force."

Shayla covered her head with her hands. "I probably could deal with reality, if that was the worst part of it."

"What could be worse than a man dead?"

"Oh, let's see, the fact that the child Rhonda is carrying could be Antonio's baby."

Lissa placed her pinkie finger into her left ear and started cleaning it out with her fingernail. When she finished that ear, she moved to the other one and started cleaning it out. "There, I'm sure I had some wax building up and I did not hear you right, so please say that again."

Agitated, Shayla jumped to her feet. "Rhonda thinks that yet another husband of mine is her baby's daddy. She sent a text to James phone after he got shot and we read it. She even said she was planning to blackmail Antonio to get money from him once the DNA test is back."

"I know you don't believe her." Lissa looked at Shayla in shock. "Do you believe her?"

"Not one word of it. Antonio is a great husband. He has been there for me through times that no one else would have stuck around. I don't believe anything Rhonda is saying about him."

"Good. Trust your gut and follow your vows, through thick and thin. What God put together, let no man put asunder. Amen." Lissa snapped her fingers as she was having a spiritual moment.

"Mrs. Jackson called this morning and told me Rhonda went into labor after she heard about the shooting. She had her baby this morning and she told the nurse she wants to list Antonio Davis as the father."

"So, her story about needing counseling and having cancer, was all of that a lie?" Lissa asked.

"I am pretty sure it is a lie."

"This girl is one big ass fruit loop," Lissa said shaking her head. What did Antonio say about the whole situation?"

"I talked some sense into him, but he is ready to go down to the hospital and go off on her. Now, I am here hoping that you can talk some sense into me. No matter who her baby's daddy is, she is disrespecting me in a way that deserves a good old fashioned beat down."

"Look, a lot has happened over the past twenty four hours. I think the best thing for you and Antonio to do is to get together and comfort each other. Stay away from all of the BS, if you can. When you are ready, you will need counseling to sort through all of this."

"We were so happy, so in love. This drama is not my life!" Shayla cried for a long time and Lissa held her in her arms.

"Tears are good. Get it all out."

"I told Mrs. Jackson we want a paternity test and she told me that Rhonda said she would be happy to do one. We're going to the hospital tomorrow to get the test done."

"Good," Lissa said. "This will all be over before you know it."

Chapter 32

Antonio

One Month Later

"This cannot be right," Antonio said as he tossed the stack of papers he read to the ground. Shayla stood quiet and emotionless as he denied being the father of the child that carried his DNA. "I am not that child's father," he said with confidence. He was standing beside the mailbox, the spot where Shayla screamed to the top of her lungs when she opened the letter.

"Numbers don't lie," she said. She was numb as she walked in a trance to the house. Once she reached the steps, she added, "And, those numbers say that without a shadow of a doubt, you are ninety nine point nine percent the father of Rhonda's child, so don't try to make a fool out of me."

Frantic at this point, he shouted, "That is not my damn baby! Shayla, you have to believe me."

She was furious, as well. "Save it for someone who wants to hear it, Antonio."

"The test must be a false positive or something. Don't you have to sleep with a woman to get her pregnant? I never slept with Rhonda."

"Oh, how I want to believe every word coming from your mouth. I want to trust you, but…"

"But, nothing Shayla! These people, James, Titus and Rhonda, have been nothing but thorns in your side all of the time you have known them. And now, because I'm married to you, they are a thorn in my side. Do not let them win with this trick. We have to stick together until we get this figured out."

She ran back down the stairs, picked up the papers and threw them at him. "It's pretty much figured out. What you need to do is figure out how your dick made it inside Rhonda's panties."

He grabbed her and told her, "I did not have any type of sexual relations with that woman."

Yanking away, she was incredulous. "Listen to you sounding like Bill Clinton versus Monica Lewinski. There was one thing both of you had in common, you both left your DNA as proof. But, come on now, Rhonda? The one person who has screwed me over more times than the IRS and you cheat, and have a baby with her. Was our family not good enough for you? Was I not good enough for you?" Shayla stormed into the house without waiting for his response.

"Our family is everything to me," he said, picking up the paternity letter and reading it again. He could not believe his eyes. According to the letter, there was a ninety nine point nine percent chance that he was Rhonda Wilson's baby daddy. He went in the house and sat at the dining room table. "This is some fabricated bull."

Shayla stood at the kitchen sink while drinking a glass of water. "Yeah, but it's your problem, not mine. It stopped being our problem when the numbers didn't come back in your favor."

"It looks like I am guilty of cheating on you, I know this. The evidence is stacked against me, but I need you to believe in me for a minute. When I say..." He stood up, walked over to his wife, and turned her face toward him. "...When I say I did not have sex with Rhonda, it is the truth. I mean think about it. I didn't even know what city she or Titus were living in, much less how to contact her. Think back nine months ago. Think back night by night. I was here. With you. As long as we have been married, I have never been out of pocket."

Logically, what he said made sense. "But, the DNA test..."

"Is a lie," he finished her sentence.

She wanted to believe him, but the last man she trusted was indeed having an affair with Rhonda. Her buzzing cell phone gave her the much needed getaway she needed from Antonio. "I have to answer that," she said, picking her cell phone up from the kitchen counter. She walked over and stood by the sink. "Hello."

"Hi, Shayla. This is Mrs. Jackson."

"Oh, hi Mrs. Jackson."

Hearing Mrs. Jackson's name, Antonio was all ears. He stood close beside Shayla mouthing, "what does she want?"

Shayla shrugged her shoulders. She asked her, "What gives me the honor of your phone call this morning?"

"I know my daughter has put you through a lot this past week. That is why I'm calling. There is more to the story of Antonio being her baby's father."

"That is what we were just discussing. The DNA papers came in the mail today."

"Well, what I'm about to tell you is not going to be easy to believe. I was at her apartment this morning helping her take care of the baby when I overheard her on the phone talking with someone about child support."

"If you called me to talk about my husband paying child support for Rhonda's baby, you are out of order and I will not discuss this with you."

"No, no. That is not why I called. I called to tell you that when I called the number back, it was some lady named Chandra from the Forge Sperm Bank."

"Why would Rhonda be talking to someone from a sperm bank?" Shayla asked.

"She sounded very friendly with the lady, as if they knew each other. She asked her if anyone found out about the artificial insemination would the courts make her pay the child support back."

"I am not following you, Mrs. Jackson. What are you saying to me?"

"I do not believe your husband slept with her. I think Rhonda got Antonio's sperm from a sperm bank. And Shayla..."

"Yeah," Shayla said, not sure if she was excited that her husband did not sleep with Rhonda or upset that she had stolen his DNA and had a child. She was both.

"It is true that Rhonda does not have cancer. I asked her doctor about it and he said she has never been diagnosed with cancer. The whole cancer story was a part of her and James' plan to get money from you and your husband. Titus didn't even know what they were up to. He is devastated by what she has done."

"Thanks for calling with this information, Mrs. Jackson," Shayla said ending the call. She stared at the device in her hand for a few seconds. "Shut the front and back door!"

"What did she say? What are Rhonda and her mother up to now?"

Shayla was stoic when she asked, "Have you ever given sperm to a sperm bank?"

"No...well yeah, but that was back in my younger days when I needed cash for school. But, what does that have to do with..." Antonio paused. The reality of Rhonda's treacherous scheme hit him.

"According to what Mrs. Jackson just told me, it's possible that Rhonda worked with someone at the sperm bank to get herself pregnant with your sperm."

They stared at each other for the longest time in shock. "How could she get my sperm?"

"She knew someone who worked at the facility and they must have done a search for your name and given it to her."

"I'll be damned if she and James were not working on the hoodwinking of a century," Antonio said. "This is un-freaking-believable."

"I know," Shayla looked at him with regret. "I'm sorry for not believing you."

"Sorry, for what? This is Rhonda and James' fault."

"I'm sorry for doubting you when I should have been on your side."

"I would be upset with you, but I am not sure that I would have reacted any differently if DNA showed Tyler to be another person's son. The worst part of this is that I have to live knowing she has a part of me in her child, and she planned to use that against you."

"I wanted things to be different with Rhonda this time. I prayed that she changed."

Antonio hugged his wife. "You did your best to work with her. The only thing we can do now is pick up the pieces of our life, put it back together, and let God sort the rest out."

The End

.

42865090R00116

Made in the USA
Charleston, SC
07 June 2015